The Joy of Jesus at Christmas

A 31-day devotional for December

JOEL BREIDENBAUGH

ISBN: 0990781631
ISBN-13: 978-0990781639

DEDICATION

I dedicate this book to the members of First Baptist Church of Sweetwater in Longwood, Florida. These dear people helped me gain a fresh look at Advent and the Christmas season. I thank God often for calling me to serve this church, for they are a great joy.

CONTENTS

ACKNOWLEDGEMENTS

A writing project is seldom the work of a single author. Scores of others helped me in various ways to have what you are reading. It behooves me to express words of gratitude to several.

First, I am indebted to First Baptist Sweetwater in Longwood, Florida. Before I ever came to serve this church, the body of believers approved a recommendation to grant 2-month sabbaticals to the full-time ministerial staff for every 5 years of service. As I approached my 5-year anniversary, I requested to take the sabbatical 3 months early and the Personnel Team was gracious in honoring my request. The staff picked up additional responsibilities while I was away, and I appreciate all they do for me and our Lord. I love shepherding the people of Sweetwater. Many of the devotions were first introduced to this church through my smaller writing projects for the church. It would have taken me years to write this book had I not used a few weeks of the sabbatical for this project.

Second, I am grateful to my alma mater, the Baptist College of Florida in Graceville, where I spent a few weeks of my sabbatical. President Tom Kinchen has done a remarkable job in leading that school. The library staff was particularly helpful, especially the director, John Shaffett, and several student employees, namely Ryan and Patricia Ayala, Jeffrey Basford, Shawn Branham, Kathryn Dukes and James Oney. They provided me a quiet place of study and allowed me to utilize many biblical, theological and musical resources. While I do not cite long lists of these materials (partly by my own understanding of the text and partly to avoid wearying the

1

reader), I did "check my work" against other scholars.

Third, God has truly blessed me with a loving and supportive family. Annthea and I met at that college in Graceville, a short distance from where she grew up. From our initial meeting in 1994 to our friendship, dating relationship, engagement and marriage, she has always supported my endeavors. She has also taught our five children—Hannah, John Mark, Alethea, Lukas and Joanna—about waiting on Daddy to get home from his work. Those kids bring great joy to our lives (our kids, along with Sia Nadtochii, our exchange student, served as a test case for these devotionals). That my wife grew up a few miles from Graceville allowed our family to visit a few weeks with my in-laws. It also permitted me an opportunity to travel fifteen minutes away to the library to do my research.

Fourth, I want to thank Cameo Eelman for cover design. She is very talented. I also am very appreciative of Tom Cheyney and Mark Weible of Renovate Publishing Group for the encouragement and helpful tips to see this work published.

Finally, words alone cannot express my eternal thankfulness to God the Father and our Lord Jesus Christ. The Lord transformed my life as a child through the faithful teaching of my parents and has demonstrated great patience in molding me into His child. God has taught me much about who He is and what He has done, and some of that understanding comes out in this book. May our Lord receive all "power and wealth and wisdom and might and honor and glory and blessing" (Revelation 5:12) now and forevermore!

Joel Breidenbaugh
September 2015

INTRODUCTION

There is no other time of the year quite like Christmas. Crowds fill streets and shops. People treat each other with more frequent smiles and greetings. Many travel great distances to see family. And hundreds of millions visit a church at Christmastime.

Why all the commotion at this time of year? Because it is the time on the calendar we have set aside to remember God fulfilling His promise to send Christ. We read about it throughout the Scriptures. This book digs into select verses from the Bible to highlight God's faithfulness. And this message isn't merely thousands of years old, but it's still applicable today. The Apostle Paul observed the following:

> For whatever was written in former days was written for our instruction, that through endurance and through the encouragement of the Scriptures we might have hope. (Romans 15:4)

> As surely as God is faithful, our word to you has not been Yes and No. For the Son of God, Jesus Christ… was not Yes and No, but in him it is always Yes. For all the promises of God find their Yes in him." (2 Corinthians 1:18-20a)

I hope you find these 31 devotions for Christmas to be an encouragement to you in God's message of "Yes" in Christ.

Because Christmas carries a multitude of meanings—promise, hope, fulfillment, joy and the like, I have grouped the readings into larger, celebratory themes. I try to share an important truth or two in each reading, helping you grow deeper in your understanding of

God's Word, so you can, in turn, grow closer to the Lord.

Moreover, in addition to the devotional reading for each day of the month, I give a few other elements to resonate with various readers. First of all, I use a poem to summarize the main idea of that day's devotion into a more memorable rhythm.

Second, I provide a popular song, usually with an element related to the devotional idea. The song is meant to turn the doctrinal truth into praise. To underscore the season of Christmas, I've included mostly popular Christmas carols or songs. In most cases, I've simply included the traditional verses, but I've also provided the original verses to a few songs. To avoid copyright infringements, all of the songs I've selected are free to the public domain (you may want to search other songs online). Since I designed these devotions for the family, I suggest you sing a capella, play an instrument, or find the accompany music online at such places as cyberhymnal.org or hymntime.com (or if you prefer not to sing, you can listen to the songs on YouTube.com or a similar site).

Third, I add an application idea each day to help you (and your family) appropriate some aspect of the biblical truth into your life. Finally, the sample prayer may aid you in your own thanksgiving to our Lord. It is my hope you find some, if not all, of these extra features beneficial in your worship of our Lord Jesus Christ.

THE PROMISE BEGUN

JOEL BREIDENBAUGH

December 1   The Promise-Maker

The LORD God said to the serpent, ". . . I will put enmity between you and the woman, and between your offspring and her offspring; He shall bruise your head, and you shall bruise his heel." (Genesis 3:14-15)

Millions, if not billions, of promises are made every single day. Often they are little things: "I'll see you at 5," or "I'll call you tonight," or the like. Sometimes promises carry significant weight, like promising to keep a marital vow for the rest of your life or agreeing to take on a new job (promising that you will perform those things which are expected of you) or promising to pay a mortgage payment. Promises can be small or big, but people make promises virtually every day.

Opening up the first pages of Scripture, we don't have to read far until we come to some of God's promises. Now, to be clear, Genesis 3:15 is not the very first promise in all of Scripture. God makes promises before that one. Whether one views God's creative commands in chapter one as "promises" (He said "'Let there be light' and there was light," which may indicate something of a "promise" that He fulfills immediately), everyone agrees that God promised death for mankind should he eat of the tree of the knowledge of good and evil (2:17). God also promised physical and spiritual union in the act of marriage (2:24). God, like people, is a Promise-*Maker*.

Genesis 3 takes a major turn, as you know. Some time has passed since God created Adam and Eve. Lucifer, known as Satan, has now fallen from his exalted state (see Isaiah 14:12-21; Ezekiel 28:12-19; cf. Revelation 12:3-9—theologians for centuries have interpreted these passages as describing Lucifer's fall). This fall did not occur much earlier, because all that God had made was called "very good" (1:31). Whenever and however Satan's fall happened, he shows up in the Garden of Eden as a serpent (see Revelation 20:2, for example, as one text that identifies the serpent of old with the devil). His plan is to challenge God through the people He created in His own image. It worked. Satan won a victory that day. He deceived Eve into doubting God's promise and Adam disobeyed God's command and man and woman *broke* their inherent promise to follow God completely. The whole human race became sinners, and promise-*breakers*, with Adam and Eve that day.

In response to mankind's rebellion, God punished Adam and Eve and removed them from the Garden, bringing spiritual death from their sin. You see, God is not simply a Promise-*Maker*, but He is also a Promise-*Keeper*. We *make* promises all the time. Some we *keep*. Some we *break*. God *keeps* all of His promises (see December 2).

This faithfulness of God is what makes Genesis 3:15 so significant. He promises Satan that a struggle will take place between him and all of Eve's offspring. Spiritual warfare has been alive and well ever since that day. That truth, however, isn't the crux of the matter. The word "seed" ("offspring") is singular in the original Hebrew. Now the singular in Hebrew can speak of a corporate unity, where it speaks of a collective bunch as one. But something more is at play here—much more. God not only promises a struggle, but He adds that the serpent will strike the heel of the seed, while the seed will crush the serpent's head. God promises Satan's defeat for the first time just moments after his apparent victory!

> So please hear God's first promise that He makes
> To defeat the snake of the life he takes,
> You should take interest in this here word—
> Now read yet more for the sake of the Lord.

Application Idea

What are some promises you have made recently? Did you keep them? What promises have been made to you? Were they kept? What's a promise you can make to a family member or friend today? Talk to them about what you will do for them. If the opportunity arises, tell them about the great promise God made in Genesis 3.

"Hark! The Herald Angels Sing"
Author: Charles Wesley, 1739

Hark! The herald angels sing,
"Glory to the newborn King;
Peace on earth, and mercy mild,
God and sinners reconciled!"

THE JOY OF JESUS AT CHRISTMAS

Joyful, all ye nations rise,
Join the triumph of the skies;
With th'angelic host proclaim,
"Christ is born in Bethlehem!"

Refrain:
Hark! the herald angels sing,
"Glory to the newborn King!"

Christ, by highest Heav'n adored;
Christ the everlasting Lord;
Late in time, behold Him come,
Offspring of a virgin's womb.
Veiled in flesh the Godhead see;
Hail th'incarnate Deity,
Pleased with us in flesh to dwell,
Jesus our Emmanuel.

Hail the heav'nly Prince of Peace!
Hail the Sun of Righteousness!
Light and life to all He brings,
Ris'n with healing in His wings.
Mild He lays His glory by,
Born that man no more may die.
Born to raise the sons of earth,
Born to give them second birth.

Come, Desire of nations, come,
Fix in us Thy humble home;
Rise, the woman's conqu'ring Seed,
Bruise in us the serpent's head.
Now display Thy saving power,
Ruined nature now restore;
Now in mystic union join
Thine to ours, and ours to Thine.

Adam's likeness, Lord, efface,
Stamp Thine image in its place:
Second Adam from above,
Reinstate us in Thy love.

Let us Thee, though lost, regain,
Thee, the Life, the inner man:
O, to all Thyself impart,
Formed in each believing heart.

Prayer

Lord, thank You for Your grace in announcing Your victory over Satan just after the Fall. May we always find great hope in all Your promises. In Jesus' name, Amen.

December 2   The Promise-Keeper

And God said, "This is the sign of the covenant that I make between me and you and every living creature that is with you, for all future generations: I have set my bow in the clouds, and it shall be a sign of the covenant between me and the earth. When I bring clouds over the earth and the bow is seen in the clouds, I will remember my covenant that is between me and you and every living creature of all flesh. And the waters shall never again become a flood to destroy all flesh. When the bow is in the clouds, I will see it and remember the everlasting covenant between God and every living creature of all flesh that is on the earth." (Genesis 9:12-16)

One of the first Bible stories kids learn is Noah and the ark. Undoubtedly its popularity with children has much to do with the animals in the story. Two land animals—a male and a female—of every kind made its way to the ark: dogs, cats, bears, frogs, snakes, lizards, elephants, monkeys, ostriches, mice, deer, cows, horses and much, much more. These animals boarded the ark to be spared the judgment of God on the earth by way of flood. We aren't just talking about a local flashflood which occurs many times annually around the world, sometimes resulting in a few deaths. Why not? Because the flood in Noah's day was far worse—it rained for 40 days *and* nights (think of an ongoing downpour) as "the windows of the heavens were opened" and water sprang up from below the earth's surface as "all the fountains of the great deep burst forth" (Genesis 7:11). The flood waters were so great "all the high mountains under the whole heaven were covered. The waters prevailed above the mountains, covering them fifteen cubits deep [more than 20 feet].... And the waters prevailed on the earth 150 days" (7:19-20, 24). That is a lot of water, far more water than a local flood!

But there's another reason why Noah's flood could not have been a local flood: because local floods happen all the time and God promised never to flood the earth again like He did in Noah's day. If the flood in Genesis 7 was a local flood, then God is a liar, because local floods are regular. If it was a worldwide flood, however, as we see in Scripture and as evidence of marine life on mountains suggests, then God is not a liar, but a truth-teller.

One of the points of the great flood is to teach the totality of God's judgment against sin. The occasion for God's judgment was when "the LORD saw that the wickedness of man was great in the earth, and that every intention of the thoughts of his heart was only evil continually" (6:5). Mankind's great evil deserved a death-sentence. Even though some people or animals may have survived a few days or weeks by floating along on pieces of wood or debris, no one would have lasted months in such a deluge. All would have died by drowning. The story of Noah and the ark is not really a happy children's story, but a fear-filled, agonizing death of the entire land population of the earth. You may not like to think of the flood this way, but you cannot deny this implication in the biblical text.

Maybe the flood serves as another reminder for us all. Like sinners present in Noah's day, our earth gets worse with each passing year. But instead of God judging us immediately through a flood, He shows mercy and patience by giving us time to think about our future death. And when we think about that subject, we begin to wonder how we can be prepared to face it.

This thought brings me to another major point of the flood narrative, the point we love to dwell on. God saved some from the flood by preserving them on the ark. He saved animals and Noah's family, so that He could start afresh with His work of re-creation (see 1 Peter 3:18-22).

But it wasn't enough for God to spare Noah and his family from the flood. God also gave Noah and mankind a promise: we wouldn't have to worry about another worldwide flood ever again. The rainbow became a sign, a symbol of God's faithfulness, reminding us that our God is not simply a Promise-Maker, but He's also a Promise-*Keeper*. That means we can trust what He says elsewhere in His Word. And that, my friend, is good news!

> All-too-often, I'm a promise-breaker.
> Thanks be to God, the great Promise-Maker
> And Keeper of ev'ry word He does give,
> And spares some people so that they might live!

Application Idea
Find a picture of a rainbow. How many colors can you see? Just as a rainbow displays multiple colors, so the Lord's faithfulness is multi-faceted to us. What are some ways God has shown His faithfulness to you?

"Standing on the Promises of God"
Author: R. Kelso Carter, 1886

Standing on the promises of Christ my King,
Through eternal ages let His praises ring,
Glory in the highest, I will shout and sing,
Standing on the promises of God.

Refrain:
Standing, standing,
Standing on the promises of God my Savior;
Standing, standing,
I'm standing on the promises of God.

Standing on the promises that cannot fail,
When the howling storms of doubt and fear assail,
By the living Word of God I shall prevail,
Standing on the promises of God.

Standing on the promises I now can see
Perfect, present cleansing in the blood for me;
Standing in the liberty where Christ makes free,
Standing on the promises of God.

Standing on the promises of Christ the Lord,
Bound to Him eternally by love's strong cord,
Overcoming daily with the Spirit's sword,
Standing on the promises of God.

Standing on the promises I cannot fall,
List'ning every moment to the Spirit's call,
Resting in my Savior as my all in all,
Standing on the promises of God.

Prayer

Our heavenly Father, Your faithfulness is never-ending. We praise You for being a God who keeps His promises. Help us live in faithfulness to You. In Jesus' name, Amen.

December 3   The Promise-Clarifier

Now the LORD said to Abram, "Go from your country and your kindred and your father's house to the land that I will show you. And I will make of you a great nation, and I will bless you and make your name great, so that you will be a blessing. I will bless those who bless you, and him who dishonors you I will curse, and in you all the families of the earth shall be blessed. . . ." Then the LORD appeared to Abram and said, "To your offspring I will give this land." (Genesis 12:1-3, 7)

Okay. So we *make* promises and *break* promises. But we *keep* some promises. We may even *reword* a promise so that it is easier for us to keep. For instance, an increasing number of marital vows taken these days are getting less specific, so that people don't feel like they are breaking a commitment to a spouse, should the need arise to "get out" of a relationship (I'm not trying to beat people up who have had divorces, for some are well within biblical permissions. I'm simply acknowledging that many weddings have watered-down the vows or promises between the two parties). Because of my propensity to forget, and therefore break, simple promises, I've been guilty of making *weak* promises. Instead of telling someone, "I'll call you back next week," I have said, "I'll talk to you soon." It may be weeks or months before I talk to him again, but I can use "soon" loosely. Any of us can *reword* our promises to justify not breaking them.

Not God. He may very well restate or *reword* or *clarify* a promise to underscore a certain element of the promise. Unlike me, however, such rewording doesn't *weaken* the promise but *strengthens* the promise. God clarifies many of His promises. He makes them more specific. He doesn't want us to miss them.

The LORD's promise to Abram (whose name changes to Abraham later) is specific. Now God doesn't tell Abram that He will cause more than 30 million Jews throughout history to come from him, but God does get specific. Here are a few of those specifics:

- ➢ Great nation—though small, who would argue that Israel hasn't been extremely significant?
- ➢ Blessing Abram and a great name—the rest of Abraham's account verifies divine blessing and three major world religions of 2-3 billion label him the father of their religion

> ➤ Divine blessing for those who bless Abraham—
> historically, those who bless Israel (Abraham's physical
> descendants) are blessed by God
> ➤ Divine cursing for those who dishonor Abraham—
> throughout history those who have fought against and
> mistreated Israel receive a bad reputation and have been
> known to face drought, famine, poverty, death and more

Not only did God promise these things, but He also established His covenant promise with Abraham and his "offspring" (see this promise repeated and emphasized in 13:15-16; 15:3, 18; 17:7-8; cf. 3:15). The Apostle Paul provides insight that God's covenant is with Abraham and his *singular* offspring/seed, Christ (Galatians 3:16; see December 1 above). To be included in God's covenant promise of greatness, blessing, and a future, you must be "in" this singular Seed.

Leave it to our Lord to strengthen His prophecy
And build up His people all throughout history.
God specifies in telling us Whom to be in.
Read on to discover deliverance from sin.

Application Idea
Look at a globe or a world map and find Israel. How big is it in comparison to other countries? Would you expect a land this size to be home to a great people? What do these insights teach you about God?

"Tell Me the Story of Jesus"
Author: Fanny Crosby, 1880

Tell me the story of Jesus,
Write on my heart every word;
Tell me the story most precious,
Sweetest that ever was heard.
Tell how the angels in chorus,
Sang as they welcomed His birth,
"Glory to God in the highest!
Peace and good tidings to earth."

Refrain:
Tell me the story of Jesus,
Write on my heart every word;
Tell me the story most precious,
Sweetest that ever was heard.

Fasting alone in the desert,
Tell of the days that are past,
How for our sins He was tempted,
Yet was triumphant at last.
Tell of the years of His labor,
Tell of the sorrow He bore;
He was despised and afflicted,
Homeless, rejected and poor.

Tell of the cross where they nailed Him,
Writhing in anguish and pain;
Tell of the grave where they laid Him,
Tell how He liveth again.
Love in that story so tender,
Clearer than ever I see;
Stay, let me weep while you whisper,
"Love paid the ransom for me."

Prayer

God, our Creator, You have certainly done a marvelous work in calling out and blessing a people for Yourself. Thank You for including us in Christ, the Seed of Abraham, in Whose name we pray, Amen.

December 4   The Promise of a Prophet

"The LORD your God will raise up for you a prophet like me from among you, from your brothers—it is to him you shall listen—just as you desired of the LORD your God at Horeb on the day of the assembly, when you said, 'Let me not hear again the voice of the LORD my God or see this great fire any more, lest I die.' And the LORD said to me, 'They are right in what they have spoken. I will raise up for them a prophet like you from among their brothers. And I will put my words in his mouth, and he shall speak to them all that I command him. And whoever will not listen to my words that he shall speak in my name, I myself will require it of him.'" (Deuteronomy 18:15-19)

Have you ever lost a key influencer in your life—father, mother, grandparent, mentor? I'm talking about the kind of person who provided guidance for you, someone who taught you about the important things of life. After Israel left Egypt, Moses had been their leader for forty years. But he wasn't just any leader, he was a prophet, the spokesman for God; he was their intermediary between God and them. Out of their fear of God, Israel begged for someone to represent God to them. They couldn't handle the glory and holiness and greatness of God demonstrated at Sinai; neither can we.

Though God is full of holiness and purity (the opposite of sin), He is also full of grace and mercy (in dealing with sinners). God didn't have to answer Israel's request, but He did. The Lord used Moses as His prophet to speak to the people. Later God would raise up other prophets to speak His Word to His people in carrying on the ministry of revelation and covenant reinforcement.

But none of them would ever exceed Moses, because he was the first one used this way and everything they said about how Israel should live would be judged in light of what Moses said in the Law. Whatever God spoke to Moses, Moses reiterated it to Israel through spoken and written instruction. Everything the succeeding prophets spoke and wrote was tested by the authentic word from Moses. Even when Jewish leaders divided over religious and doctrinal issues in later centuries, as seen in the formation of the Pharisees and Sadducees (to name only two groups), these primary groups debated whether the latter prophets wrote God's Word. They never debated, however, the veracity of Moses' writings, because they were in agreement about its divine origin.

With this basic understanding of the prophetic ministry in mind, you can begin to see why Moses' words in Deuteronomy 18 are so important. While God spoke through Moses about future prophets as His representatives and intermediaries, He had in view a Supreme Prophet, greater than the rest, including Moses himself. This Prophet must be Jewish and speak for God with an authority which exceeds Moses.

When Jesus came to earth, people were "astonished at his teaching, for he was teaching them as one who had authority" (Matthew 7:28-29). At His words others declared "This really is the Prophet" (John 7:40)! Indeed, Jesus spoke God's Word to people and through His death and resurrection He became the ultimate Intermediary we desperately need.

Who could have guessed about this One Prophet Supreme,
And all He would say and then do—this, who could dream?
Never did He once sin, but on the contrary,
He died-yet-lives as our Intermediary!

Application Idea

Buy a package of candy canes and share them with your family. Just as Jesus was a Great Prophet and Teacher, so the candy cane can teach us a few truths about Christ. Its traditional colors are white (symbolizing Christ's righteousness) and red (a sign of His blood-sacrifice). It is hard like a rock, reminding us of the need to build our lives on Christ the Solid Rock. It is shaped like a shepherd's staff, emphasizing Jesus as the Good Shepherd watching after His sheep. Finally, the sweet flavor points to the sweet nature of Christ's saving work. What's your favorite part of the candy cane? Why?

"Praise Him! Praise Him!"
Author: Fanny Crosby, 1869

Praise Him! Praise Him! Jesus, our blessed Redeemer!
Sing, O earth, His wonderful love proclaim!
Hail Him! Hail Him! Highest archangels in glory,
Strength and honor give to His holy name!
Like a shepherd, Jesus will guard His children;
In His arms He carries them all day long.

Refrain
Praise Him! Praise Him!
Tell of His excellent greatness!
Praise Him! Praise Him!
Ever in joyful song!

Praise Him! Praise Him! Jesus, our blessed Redeemer!
For our sins He suffered, and bled, and died;
He our Rock, our hope of eternal salvation,
Hail Him! Hail Him! Jesus the crucified.
Sound His praises! Jesus who bore our sorrows,
Love unbounded, wonderful, deep and strong!

Praise Him! Praise Him! Jesus, our blessed Redeemer!
Heav'nly portals loud with hosannas ring!
Jesus, Savior, reigneth forever and ever;
Crown Him! Crown Him! Prophet and Priest and King!
Christ is coming, over the world victorious;
Power and glory unto the Lord belong!

Prayer

Lord Jesus, thank You for fulfilling the promise of God's greatest
Prophet. You faithfully spoke God's Word and taught us how to
live before God through You and Your work on the cross. We
praise you for Who You are and for what You did. In Jesus' name,
Amen.

December 5   **The Promise of the Impossible**

"Therefore the Lord himself will give you a sign. Behold, the virgin shall conceive and bear a son, and shall call his name Immanuel." (Isaiah 7:14)

Few joys in life exceed the birth of a child. Whether a couple has their first child or fifth, exceedingly great joy and happiness almost always accompany a newborn's entrance into this world. While many children are born to married parents, some are born out of wedlock. Regardless of the marital status of an infant's parents, we know virgins don't get pregnant... *ever*! Virgin births are impossible. That is why it is so easy to reject the literal reading of this verse. Surely Isaiah wasn't thinking clearly or he misunderstood what the Lord was saying to him. Or maybe there is another explanation.

Many scholars point out the word virgin could mean "young woman," but even if it means "virgin," a rational understanding follows. Even though Isaiah already had one son, the rest of the context of Isaiah 7-8 points to a possible second marriage (after his first wife passed away) to a young woman who had been a virgin and she had a son (734 BC). This son became a "sign" to foolish King Ahaz and Judah that God would give Judah over to her enemies, the Syrian-Ephraim alliance, for a few years, but by the time Isaiah's son was twelve (becoming an adult), the enemy would no longer be in the picture (722 BC). This view of virgin or young woman finds immediate fulfillment in the biblical text at hand.

That view certainly is one way to look at the prophecy of a virgin birth, but what if God meant something more. Much like an iceberg reveals only a small portion of the whole, some Old Testament prophecies with early fulfillments are simply the top of the iceberg. A deeper, greater fulfillment lies ahead. God must have intended something more in Isaiah 7 because He uses the word "behold," an attention-getter. Moreover, the "sign" that an actual "virgin shall conceive" highlights the miraculous, for the word for "virgin" is never used of a married woman. Thus, Isaiah's marriage and sexual relations mean his wife wasn't a virgin when she conceived. Furthermore, the prophecy includes bearing "a Son"— not just a child but a male child. Additionally, the phrase "shall call his name" in Hebrew is literally "she will name him," which was out of the ordinary for a mother to name her child. But if the Son didn't have a biological father, shouldn't a mother be the only one with the naming rights? Finally, the Son's name, how others would know Him, would be "Immanuel," meaning "God with us."

This virgin-born Son is far greater than Isaiah's son. If He isn't Isaiah's son, whose Son is He? He is none other than Jesus of Nazareth, who was born to a virgin, Mary (Matthew 1:20-25). Joseph would keep his betrothal intact "but knew her not until she had given birth to a son" (1:25).

"Impossible," you say. I agree. But I also know God can do the impossible (see Luke 1:34-37).

> The impossible, they say, can never be done,
> Unless, of course, it is done by the only One
> Who created th' laws of nature for all of us
> But can also intervene with the miraculous.

Application Idea
Get out a few strands of used Christmas lights. What's the probability all the lights will be working when you plug them into the socket? Impossible? What are some other impossible things you can think of? How do you value our Lord as the God of the impossible?

"O Come, O Come, Emmanuel"
Origin: Old Latin; Translators:
John M. Neale & Henry S. Coffin, 1851

O come, O come, Emmanuel,
And ransom captive Israel,
That mourns in lonely exile here
Until the Son of God appear.

Refrain:
Rejoice! Rejoice!
Emmanuel
Shall come to thee, O Israel.

O come, Thou Wisdom from on high,
Who orderest all things mightily;
To us the path of knowledge show,

21

And teach us in her ways to go.

O come, Thou Rod of Jesse, free
Thine own from Satan's tyranny;
From depths of hell Thy people save,
And give them victory over the grave.

O come, Thou Day-spring, come and cheer
Our spirits by Thine advent here;
Disperse the gloomy clouds of night,
And death's dark shadows put to flight.

O come, Thou Key of David, come,
And open wide our heavenly home;
Make safe the way that leads on high,
And close the path to misery.

O come, O come, great Lord of might,
Who to Thy tribes on Sinai's height
In ancient times once gave the law
In cloud and majesty and awe.

O come, Thou Root of Jesse's tree,
An ensign of Thy people be;
Before Thee rulers silent fall;
All peoples on Thy mercy call.

O come, Desire of nations, bind
In one the hearts of all mankind;
Bid Thou our sad divisions cease,
And be Thyself our King of Peace.

Prayer

We magnify You, Lord, Maker of heaven and earth, for being a God who can do the impossible. Help us never to doubt You but to grow in our trust of You. We pray these things in Jesus' name, Amen.

December 6   **The Promise of a Birthplace**

"But you, O Bethlehem Ephrathah, who are too little to be among the clans of Judah, from you shall come forth for me one who is to be ruler in Israel, whose coming forth is from of old, from ancient days. Therefore he shall give them up until the time when she who is in labor has given birth.... [The people of Israel] shall dwell secure, for now he shall be great to the ends of the earth. And he shall be their peace." (Micah 5:2-3a, 4b-5a)

We've all heard the Christmas carol, "O Little Town of Bethlehem," a song sung in thousands of churches throughout our land. It may seem a bit odd to some that we would make such a big deal over a village worthy of the motto: "Tiny Town, Nowhere." After all, we could compose and sing lyrics about thousands of cities much larger than Bethlehem. What's the big deal?

Bethlehem, situated six miles south of Israel's capital city, Jerusalem, has been associated with David, former King of Israel. The short story of Ruth takes place primarily in Bethlehem. Ruth finds her way into the sacred pages of Scripture because she bore a son named Obed, who would become the grandfather of David. A few decades later during the tumultuous days of Saul's kingship-turned-sour, the Lord sent the prophet Samuel with these words: "I will send you to Jesse the Bethlehemite, for I have provided for myself a king among his sons" (1 Samuel 16:1). That chosen one was David, who became Israel's greatest king. His hometown of Bethlehem would hold a special place both in history, and later, in prophecy.

When Micah delivered his oracles in the late eighth century BC, he cited Bethlehem, calling to mind David's humble origin while prophesying of a ruler to be born, a ruler marked by greatness and peace. Now to be sure, many critics of the Bible reject any reference to childbirths as prophetic, for billions of women have given birth throughout history. Micah is much more precise, however, for he says that God will usher in a new era of peace for His people with this future ruler. Back in those days, the evil nation of Assyria was besieging the northern kingdom of Israel, who would soon become an oppressed people. In His goodness and grace, the Lord promised to send help from the southern kingdom of Judah. Such help would "for me" (God), i.e. one who is on God's side. This one would also "be ruler in Israel," signifying that even with a divided kingdom, the Lord desires to unite His people in peace.

Laying His cards out on the table, the Lord revealed through Micah just who this ruler would be: His origin is "from of old, from ancient days." This description is highly significant. Literally, it says that this ruler's origin is "from old, from days *eternal*." The wording is reminiscent of Moses' prayer, "from everlasting to everlasting you are God" (Psalm 90:2). A more literal rendering is "from eternal (past) to eternal (future) [or "from eternity (past) to eternity (future)] you are God." God is the great "I AM," self-existent, outside of time (see Exodus 3:14). We call Him "Yahweh," or "the LORD" (all caps in English versions mean God's personal name occurs).

The Lord promised His people over 2,700 years ago that He would send to the tiny town of Bethlehem a ruler who has existed from eternity past. Since God is the only One who existed before time began, He must be talking about Himself. Moreover, rulers of nations in ancient times were kings, so the Lord will relate to His children as a king relates to his people. Deity and royalty wrapped up in the same figure of history. Almost sounds too good to be true. Then again, it is good news.

> But how in the world can all of this truly be?
> Would the Lord Himself intervene in history?
> What of a man named Joseph and his wife Mary
> Traveling from Nazareth and become weary
> To the city of David, known as Bethlehem,
> And give birth to a son and then they swaddled him?*
> And about this tiny lil' town, why sing a song?
> Those are great questions, my friend, now read on, read on!
> *See Luke 2:4-7

Application Idea

Pick up a local newspaper or visit a news website (msn.com, foxnews.com, yahoo.com). How many "bad" news stories can you count? How many "good" news stories do you see? In a world where bad news almost always outnumbers good news, think of the good news of Christ's coming in light of a sin-saturated world. How does such news give you hope?

"O Little Town of Bethlehem"
Author: Phillips Brooks, 1867

O little town of Bethlehem, how still we see thee lie!
Above thy deep and dreamless sleep the silent stars go by.
Yet in thy dark streets shineth the everlasting Light;
The hopes and fears of all the years are met in thee tonight.

For Christ is born of Mary, and gathered all above,
While mortals sleep, the angels keep their watch of wond'ring love.
O morning stars, together proclaim the holy birth,
And praises sing to God the King, and peace to men on earth!

How silently, how silently, the wondrous Gift is giv'n;
So God imparts to human hearts the blessings of His Heav'n.
No ear may hear His coming, but in this world of sin,
Where meek souls will receive Him still, the dear Christ enters in.

Where children pure and happy pray to the blessed Child,
Where misery cries out to Thee, Son of the mother mild;
Where charity stands watching and faith holds wide the door,
The dark night wakes, the glory breaks, and Christmas comes once
more.

O holy Child of Bethlehem, descend to us, we pray;
Cast out our sin, and enter in, be born in us today.
We hear the Christmas angels the great glad tidings tell;
Oh, come to us, abide with us, our Lord Emmanuel!

Prayer
For all of Your wonders, O Lord, You are to be praised, especially
for predicting and fulfilling the birth of the Messiah, the God-
Ruler, from the little town of Bethlehem. Help us to marvel at
Your great works, and this we pray in Jesus' name, Amen.

JOEL BREIDENBAUGH

HINTS OF THE PROMISED ONE

JOEL BREIDENBAUGH

December 7   The Mystery of the Angel of Yahweh

Then he said, "Your name shall no longer be called Jacob, but Israel, for you have striven with God and with men, and have prevailed." Then Jacob asked him, "Please tell me your name." But he said, "Why is it that you ask my name?" And there he blessed him. So Jacob called the name of the place Peniel, saying, "For I have seen God face to face, and yet my life has been delivered."(Genesis 32:28-30)

My oldest daughter loves mysteries—*Nancy Drew* and "Dr. Who," to name but two. She probably got her affection for mysteries from me. But she and I are not unique in that sense, for a whole host of people enjoys a good mystery. One of the things I love about the Bible is its variety of literary genres—narrative, history, biography, law, poetry, wisdom, prophecy, gospel, epistle, apocalyptic… and *mystery*. Some mysteries are revealed in Scripture through progressive revelation—God reveals more of the mystery as time goes on—but not all of them. Some mysteries will not be solved until we stand face-to-face with the Lord. I want you to consider one mystery of Scripture with me: who is the Angel of the LORD (Angel of Yahweh) or who did Jacob wrestle with at Peniel?

Although Genesis records "a man wrestled with [Jacob]" (32:24), Hosea informs us about Jacob: "in his manhood he strove with God. He strove with the angel and prevailed; he wept and sought his favor. He met God at Bethel, and there God spoke with us—the LORD, the God of hosts, the LORD is his memorial name" (12:3b-5). So Hosea notes Jacob's wrestling with God, also described as the Angel. This revelation should not surprise us too much, for Jacob believed he saw "God face to face."

But this piece of information is only part of the mystery; the other part is the name the Angel of Yahweh did not provide to Jacob. His question "Why is it that you ask my name?" could be construed as "don't you realize who I am?"

In a separate account, Manoah, Samson's father, did not know he was talking with the Angel of the LORD and asked Him, "What is your name, so that, when your words come true, we may honor you?" And the angel of the LORD said to him, "Why do you ask my name, seeing it is wonderful?" Afterwards, "Manoah knew that he was the angel of the LORD. And Manoah said to his wife, "We shall surely die, for we have seen God" (Judges 13:16-18, 21-22).

Manoah asked the same question of the Angel of Yahweh as Jacob had and he received the same response with an additional "seeing it is wonderful." Just like Jacob, Manoah realized he had seen God. Unlike Jacob, he received additional revelation about God: One who is Wonderful (see December 14 below).

So Who is this Angel of the LORD? Is He simply a chief messenger of Yahweh? It seems He is divine, because Jacob recognized he saw God's face, as did Manoah. Could the Angel of the LORD be the pre-incarnate Christ (that is, Christ manifesting Himself before His incarnation as Jesus)? Though the Scriptures are silent about a direct connection, it seems to be a valid possibility. After all, Jesus is certainly divine and He is Wonderful!

The Bible contains a good bit of history
And doesn't disappoint with notes of mystery—
The hints of Christ's greatness and what He's all about
Let's continue reading so that we can find out.

Application Idea

Play a mystery game with your family or friends (if you don't own any popular board games, perform an online search of mystery games or mystery games for kids). What do you like about a mystery? Is the mystery about the exact nature of the Angel of Yahweh interesting to you? Why or why not?

"Silent Night, Holy Night"
Author: Joseph Mohr, 1816

Silent night, holy night,
All is calm, all is bright
Round yon virgin mother and Child.
Holy Infant, so tender and mild,
Sleep in heavenly peace,
Sleep in heavenly peace.

Silent night, holy night,
Shepherds quake at the sight;
Glories stream from heaven afar,
Heavenly hosts sing Alleluia!

Christ the Savior is born,
Christ the Savior is born!

Silent night, holy night,
Son of God, love's pure light;
Radiant beams from Thy holy face
With the dawn of redeeming grace,
Jesus, Lord, at Thy birth,
Jesus, Lord, at Thy birth.

Silent night, holy night
Wondrous star, lend thy light;
With the angels let us sing,
Alleluia to our King;
Christ the Savior is born,
Christ the Savior is born!

Prayer

Father, thank You for providing us with Your Word in a vast array of genres. You know us intimately and what peaks our interests. We praise You for opening our eyes to the mystery of the gospel and Your wonderful gift of salvation in Christ, in Whose name we pray, Amen.

December 8   For It's One, Two, Three Strikes, You're...

"For I know that my Redeemer lives, and at the last he will stand upon the earth." (Job 19:25)

No matter how much pain you've experienced, let's face it: aside from Jesus on the cross, no one has suffered more than Job. Living in the time of the patriarchs, Job "was blameless and upright, one who feared God and turned away from evil" (1:1; cf. 1:8; 2:3). God had blessed him with a good wife, ten wonderful children, good health and an enormous estate. Then, without any clear explanation, God took it all away at the request of Satan. Job lost his animals, his children and his health, and to top it all off, his wife advised him to "Curse God and die" (2:9)! Yet Job did not sin in his response to credit God with giving and taking away (1:20-22; 2:10).

If all that was not enough, three of Job's friends came to "comfort" him by accusing him of every sin under the sun. Job's replies are a mixture of disbelief, discouragement and cries to God. In these pleas we find Job's great desire: an umpire to represent both God and man.

In the first set of speeches between Job and his friends, Job admitted, "If one wished to contend with him, one could not answer him once in a thousand times" (9:3). In ancient days, there were two basic ways to win court cases. One way was to out-argue your opponent. The other way was to wrestle your adversary. Job knew he didn't stand a chance against God either way! Job exclaimed, "He is not a man, as I am, that I might answer him, that we should come to trial together. There is no arbiter between us, that might his hand on us both" (9:32-33). You get the sense Job desperately wanted such an arbiter or heavenly umpire to bring reconciliation between God and him.

By the second series of conversations, Job apparently grew in his understanding of a heavenly advocate. Because his earthly loyalists had failed, Job cried, "Even now, behold, my witness is in heaven, and he who testifies for me is on high... that he would argue the case of a man with God, as a son of man does with his neighbor" (16:19, 21). Job believed the witness and defender he needed resided only in heaven. Such an arbiter is like an interpreter between two parties who don't speak the same language.

When you consider these texts together, it seems clear Job was looking to God to defend him, much like the prologue reveals God arguing in Job's favor against Satan. While God's actions against Job made him appear guilty of great sin (as argued by Job's friends), Job trusted God's character to defend him.

Along these same lines, Job became deeply convinced the Lord would come to his aid. In light of all his troubles, he announced his belief in Yahweh as Redeemer (19:25). The term *redeemer* occurs 44 times in the Old Testament. It was a protector or legal preserver for a close relative. The redeemer could redeem a relative's property (cf. Leviticus 25:23-25; Ruth 4:4-15), avenge a slain relative (Numbers 35:19-27), marry a brother's childless widow (Ruth 4:10), purchase a relative out of slavery (Leviticus 25:47-55) or defend a relative's cause in a lawsuit (Psalm 119:154; Proverbs 23:11). The word also serves as one of Yahweh's titles (Exodus 6:6; Psalms 74:2; Isaiah 41:14).

Was Job experiencing progressive theology, learning more about God through his trials? Is Job's call for a judge/umpire, witness, advocate and arbiter the same as this Redeemer? It appears to be, and the Redeemer taking His "stand upon the earth" is a technical legal term meaning to "stand up" as a witness in court. By the end of the story, God "stands up" for Job against his friends (42:7-9).

Job's final plea for such a defense attorney occurs at the end of the third and final cycle of speeches. Desperately wanting to be heard, he cried, "Oh, that I had one to hear me! (Here is my signature! Let the Almighty answer me!) Oh, that I had the indictment written by my adversary!" (31:35). Job had grown frustrated by his friends' constant, unfounded rebukes. He wanted a judge to answer him, even God. A short while later, God spoke to Job but He didn't explain why Job had suffered. The Lord, however, demonstrated His greatness and Job responded with repentance and silence.

When you take time to add up the parts of Job's request for a heavenly Defender who could represent both God and him, it seems obvious Job needed a God-Man to serve as Judge. God had such an Advocate in mind, ready to be revealed at a later time. Christ is the Redeemer we all need, heaven's Umpire. And He's worth trusting, because He never misses a call.

Have you ever felt like you were wrongly accused?
Have you watched the guilty go free and be excused?
And how will God judge you—immoral, thief and liar?
You best flee to your Advocate, heaven's Umpire.

Application Idea

Go to a ball game or watch one on TV. Why is it important to have
officials at the game? What if you removed the officials? How do
officials help mediate a game? How is Christ a Mediator between
God and man? How does He represent both sides?

"How Great Our Joy"
Origin: Traditional German Carol, Late 19th century

> While by the sheep we watched at night,
> Glad tidings brought an angel bright.
>
> Refrain:
> How great our joy! (Great our joy!)
> Joy, joy, joy! (Joy, joy, joy!)
> Praise we the Lord in heav'n on high!
> (Praise we the Lord in heav'n on high!)
>
> There shall be born, so He did say,
> In Bethlehem a Child today.
>
> There shall the Child lie in a stall,
> This Child who shall redeem us all.
>
> This gift of God we'll cherish well,
> That ever joy our hearts shall fill.

Prayer

We exalt you, O God, for providing us a Redeemer in Jesus Christ.
He is our Advocate and Helper, the perfect Mediator and Umpire
between God and us. We offer up this praise in His name, Amen.

December 9   **God Can Use Any Ole Fool to Do His Work**

"The oracle of Balaam the son of Beor, the oracle of the man whose eye is opened, the oracle of him who hears the words of God, and knows the knowledge of the Most High, who sees the vision of the Almighty, falling down with his eyes uncovered: I see him, but not now; I behold him, but not near: a star shall come out of Jacob, and a scepter shall rise out of Israel; it shall crush the forehead of Moab and break down all the sons of Sheth. Edom shall be dispossessed; Seir also, his enemies, shall be dispossessed. Israel is doing valiantly. And one from Jacob shall exercise dominion and destroy the survivors of cities!" (Numbers 24:15-19)

Winston Churchill said, "The greatest lesson in life is to know that even fools are right sometimes." That piece of wisdom surely applies to the false prophet Balaam. As Moses led Israel through the wilderness toward the Promised Land, they defeated the Amorites and began to encounter the Moabites. Balak, king of Moab, hired the diviner Balaam to curse Israel. As foolish as Balaam was (not only did he practice divination but he also later enticed Israel to sexual immorality and idolatry, 31:16), he had just enough sense to consult Yahweh about cursing Israel. Through multiple inquires of the LORD and after God humbled Balaam by way of his donkey, Balaam learned to speak only what God put in his mouth and, instead of cursing Israel, blessed Israel through four oracles. Each oracle adds new insight into the character of God and His plan for His people. Balaam saved His best blessing for last.

Balaam begins by recognizing God as the Giver of the oracles and, ultimately, blessings. God is the Most High (higher than the false gods of Moab and the ancient Near East) and the Almighty. None can thwart what God says, for He is greater than all.

The phrases "I see him, but not now; I behold him, but not near" refer to a distant fulfillment of this prophecy. The references to *star* and *scepter* point to the *glory* and *power* of a king, respectively, implying the future of Israel includes a kingdom. Such news was not at all welcomed by Balak, king of Moab, because instead of running Israel off into another land, he learned Israel would become a kingdom, and not just any kingdom, but the kingdom which would "crush the forehead of Moab!"

A few hundred years passed after Balaam's prophecy and the

rule of King David. David was a great warrior, leading Israel to defeat the Philistines, Edomites, Moabites, Ammonites and more (2 Samuel 8:1-15). With all of David's victories, it is easy to see him as the fulfillment of this prophecy.

But could Balaam's prophecy have been even *more distant* than first realized? One thousand years after King David, a group of astrologers traveled from the east to Jerusalem. They sought the answer to what they had witnessed: "Where is he who has been born king of the Jews? For we saw His star when it rose and have come to worship him" (Matthew 2:2). Could this reference to a star (glory) and kingship (scepter, power) cause these astrologers to give up their futile and foolish religious ways? Could this star point to a King greater than David as the ultimate fulfillment of a fool's prophecy?

> News about great and powerful and future kings
> And all the expectant hope which that truly brings
> Along with a bright star, may indicate glory
> And help readers in understanding Christ's story.

Application Idea

Step outside at night and look up into the starry sky. Do any stars stand out? Why? Would a bright, moving star that suddenly stopped get your attention? How else does God use nature to teach us about Him?

"Sing We Now of Christmas"
Origin: Traditional French Carol, 15th century

Sing we now of Christmas, Noel, sing we here!
Hear our grateful praises to the Babe so dear.

Refrain:
Sing we Noel, the King is born, Noel!
Sing we now of Christmas, sing we now Noel!

Angels called to shepherds, "Leave your flocks at rest;
Journey forth to Bethl'hem, find the Lambkin blest."

In the stall they found Him; Joseph and Mary mild
Seated 'round the manger, watching the holy Child.

From the eastern country came the kings afar,
Bearing gifts to Bethl'hem, guided by a star.

Gold and myrrh they took there, gifts of greatest price;
There was ne'er a stable so like paradise.

Prayer

We stand amazed at Your mighty power, Lord, and the many ways
You have taught people to learn about You and Your special plan
in Jesus. Help us never lose our awe of You. We pray in Jesus'
name, Amen.

December 10   **The Wise Shepherd**

The words of the wise are like goads, and like nails firmly fixed are the collected sayings; they are given by one Shepherd. (Ecclesiastes 12:11)

Of all the schools in this world, they really boil down to two kinds and we've probably all attended both of them. One is the traditional school where students learn from a teacher about a variety of subjects. The other is the school of hard-knocks where individuals take on life and get a whipping. Both schools have something to teach us, and people can gain wisdom from either school, if they listen and learn.

When we think about wisdom, we could be led astray, because we have been conditioned to think primarily of a sage or an aged, spiritual guru. Now, to be sure, the wise in the verse above refers to a spiritual counselor, one of the three great institutions of ministry in the Old Testament. Jeremiah says, "The law shall not perish from the priest, nor counsel from the wise, nor the word from the prophet" (18:18).

But wisdom is not usually about a class of spiritual intellectuals, but about *knowing* what is right and *doing* it. God punished Judah because, even though they had "the law of the LORD.... The wise men shall be put to shame; they shall be dismayed and taken; behold, they have rejected the word of the LORD, so what wisdom is in them?" (Jeremiah 8:8-9). Judah knew what was right but failed to do it, proving they weren't really wise at all.

That "the words of the wise are like goads" means the wisdom literature of the Bible (Proverbs, Ecclesiastes, some Psalms, etc.) is not simply to be known, but *lived.* The metaphor of a goad refers to farmers prodding cattle, sheep or oxen by means of persuasion, much like spurs are used in riding a horse or camel. These wise sayings provide moral instruction and guidance, persuading any who will listen.

Moreover, wisdom from similar sources are "like nails firmly fixed," which means the true wisdom from God through teachers is strong, sturdy, fixed and hard to move. The tent peg is probably in mind and elsewhere the tent peg is synonymous with the cornerstone from Judah, both referring to the future Messiah as One who is stable and necessary for a strong foundation in life (cf.

Zechariah 10:3-4).

Finally, the wise sayings and masters of collections come from one Shepherd. Jewish readers would be very familiar with the Psalmists' analogy of Yahweh as a caring and protective Shepherd (23:1; 80:1). In light of the connections with the goad and tent peg/nail, the reader sees the one Shepherd equipped to direct His flock and fix His place among them. Surely this is no hired hand which runs at the sound of trouble. No, He is a Good Shepherd, ready to lay "down his life for the sheep" (John 10:11).

> History and mystery and greatness galore!
> Did anyone ever know all God had in store?
> He used a star to signal to the men so wise
> And spoke through a donkey to open Balaam's eyes.
> An Advocate from heaven was Job's only hope,
> His precious Redeemer, and the life-saving rope.
> Now here is some wisdom both to know and to do:
> Trust the Good Shepherd, because He surely loves you!

Application Idea

Search online for some pictures of sheep, or if you live near some sheep, take a drive. Let your children make sheep sounds. What are some things shepherds must do for their sheep? In what ways does the Lord provide for you like a shepherd? Ask your children what would happen to them if you went to a crowded place and were not paying attention to them? How is parental care like a shepherd? How is God's ability and care greater than what a parent can do?

"O Come, All Ye Faithful"
Author: John F. Reading, c. 1751;
Translator: Frederick Oakeley, 1841

O come, all ye faithful, joyful and triumphant,
O come ye, O come ye, to Bethlehem.
Come and behold Him, born the King of angels;

Refrain
O come, let us adore Him,
O come, let us adore Him,

O come, let us adore Him,
Christ the Lord.

True God of true God, Light from Light Eternal,
Lo, He shuns not the Virgin's womb;
Son of the Father, begotten, not created;

Sing, choirs of angels, sing in exultation;
O sing, all ye citizens of heaven above!
Glory to God, all glory in the highest;

See how the shepherds, summoned to His cradle,
Leaving their flocks, draw nigh to gaze;
We too will thither bend our joyful footsteps;

Lo! star led chieftains, Magi, Christ adoring,
Offer Him incense, gold, and myrrh;
We to the Christ Child bring our hearts' oblations.

Child, for us sinners poor and in the manger,
We would embrace Thee, with love and awe;
Who would not love Thee, loving us so dearly?

Prayer

Jesus, You are our Good Shepherd. You have taught us wisdom in living by faith and You faithfully protect us from danger. Thank You for Your loving care, and it is in Your name we pray, Amen.

ANNOUNCING THE PROMISE OF THE KING

JOEL BREIDENBAUGH

December 11   **Worthy of Worship and Praise**

"Judah, your brothers shall praise you; your hand shall be on the neck of your enemies; your father's sons shall bow down before you. Judah is a lion's cub; from the prey, my son, you have gone up. He stooped down; he crouched as a lion and as a lioness; who dares rouse him? The scepter shall not depart from Judah, nor the ruler's staff from between his feet, until tribute comes to him; and to him shall be the obedience of the peoples." (Genesis 49:8-10)

Have you ever noticed that last words are often lasting words? People usually remember the final words of a loved one, whether they are words of love, affirmation, commitment or promise. One's final words can offer hope to the next generation.

At the end of Jacob's life, he gathered his twelve sons around him to offer words of prophecy concerning their (and their tribes') future. Some words contained judgment; some words contained hope. The promise about Judah and his descendants stands out among the rest: all the rest of Israel would praise Judah, for from him would arise rulers, strong rulers like a lion.

A scepter belongs in the hands of only one kind of person: a ruler. The ruler may govern a local town or region or country or empire, but he rules over others. How strong and powerful a ruler and his people are determines the vastness of his reign.

Furthermore, these rulers would establish laws, for the word *staff* literally carries the idea of engraving or inscribing a law. The notion of pairing scepter and staff together conveys a strong authority figure, one who makes laws and leads the way in following such laws.

Because of this prophecy, it was no surprise to the Jewish people when God sent Samuel to anoint David to replace Saul as King of Israel, for David was from the tribe of Judah (cf. 1 Chronicles 2:4-15). David and his sons sat on the throne over Israel and/or Judah over 400 years. But then it came to an end with the Babylonians, followed by the Medo-Persians, then the Greeks and Romans. The saying "All good things must come to an end" seemed true for the once-great Kingdom of Israel.

The Jews, however, know about the character of God, who does not lie. Thus, they view Jacob's promise to Judah as prophetic concerning the coming Messiah. The Messiah has the right to enact laws and govern His people. This Messiah must come from Judah through the line of David, for God inspired Jacob with this prophetic word. A couple of clues in the text lead to this understanding.

First, Jacob says of Judah and his representative(s): "your brothers shall praise you." *Praise* is almost always reserved for God in the Old Testament, especially when one joins it with *bowing* (prostrating, laying low). Praise + bowing = worship. Will this praise and worship point beyond Judah to David or could it point even further to One greater than David, like the Son of David, the Messiah?

Second, the Hebrew phrase translated "until" in verse 10 occurs four other times in the Old Testament (Genesis 26:13; 41:49; 2 Samuel 23:10; 2 Chronicles 26:15). Each time indicates a climax in the narrative, for Joseph stored so much grain *until* it could no longer be measured (Gen 41:49) and David killed so many Philistines *until* his hand got weary (2 Sam 23:10). Therefore, the rule and reign will not depart from Judah *until* it climaxes in the "tribute comes to him." Many scholars agree this phrase refers to the authority of the coming ruler. While David was a great king, even the Jews expect Messiah to be a greater king, for He will be the climactic ruler from Judah over all of His people.

When we begin to add things together about this prophecy, we look for "the Lion of the tribe of Judah," who should come from "the Root of David" (Revelation 5:5), to have the strength and ability to rule and to Whom worship is due. That is the Messiah we look for and desperately need to rule our lives!

It is natural to bow down before a king,
But worship belongs to God—to Him we must cling,
And sing our songs full of adoration and praise
To the Lion of Judah throughout all our days.

Application Idea

Get down on the floor and practice bowing. When you bow before another, what does it say about you? What does it signify about the person to whom you bow? How should our lives be lived in such worship of our Lord?

"Angels, from the Realms of Glory"
Author: James Montgomery, 1816

Angels from the realms of glory,
Wing your flight o'er all the earth;
Ye who sang creation's story
Now proclaim Messiah's birth.

Refrain:
Come and worship, come and worship,
Worship Christ, the newborn King.

Shepherds, in the field abiding,
Watching o'er your flocks by night,
God with us is now residing;
Yonder shines the infant light:

Sages, leave your contemplations,
Brighter visions beam afar;
Seek the great Desire of nations;
Ye have seen His natal star.

Saints, before the altar bending,
Watching long in hope and fear;
Suddenly the Lord, descending,
In His temple shall appear.

Sinners, wrung with true repentance,
Doomed for guilt to endless pains,
Justice now revokes the sentence,
Mercy calls you; break your chains.

Though an Infant now we view Him,
He shall fill His Father's throne,
Gather all the nations to Him;
Every knee shall then bow down:

All creation, join in praising
God, the Father, Spirit, Son,

Evermore your voices raising
To th'eternal Three in One.

Prayer

Heavenly Father, grant me the right spirit of worship in praise and adoration of You and the One You sent, Jesus Christ, the Lion from the tribe of Judah and Root of David. Let my life be one of bowing before You, and I make this request in Jesus' name, Amen.

December 12   **Redeeming the Outcast**

"Blessed be the LORD, who has not left you this day without a redeemer, and may his name be renowned in Israel!" "...A son has been born to Naomi." They named him Obed. He was the father of Jesse, the father of David. (Ruth 4:14, 17)

Have you ever felt like an outsider? Maybe you weren't part of a particular clique or you were the last one chosen for a team or you just didn't quite fit in with others. You may know what it feels like to be an outcast, like you don't belong. Don't let it worry you, because some of God's greatest people didn't initially fit their surroundings.

Let's journey back more than 3,000 years to a tiny village called Bethlehem, a name which literally means "house of bread." A misfortune occurs in that land, for there was a famine (no bread, talk about irony!). A man named Elimelech takes his wife Naomi and their two boys and they travel east into enemy territory— Moab—to make a living. Then tragedy strikes, for Elimelech dies. Because life must go on, both sons eventually take wives there. Added to the misfortune of leaving their homeland and the tragedy of Naomi losing her husband, a full-blown catastrophe happens— Naomi's sons die! In ancient Jewish society, a woman's security, source of income, livelihood, life itself, was tied up in the men of her family. It began with her father, transferred to her husband at marriage, and finally centered in her sons or sons-in-law toward the end of life. Naomi's life—her real living—came to an end with the loss of her husband and sons. She became bitter toward Yahweh and had no reason to live.

Let's face it. Life can stink. Rotten things happen to good people. Friendships divide. People lose jobs. Banks foreclose on homes. Cancer evades perfectly healthy lives. Death strikes at those closest to us. When such events occur, we can get bitter. Even at God. We may think we have no real reason to live.

In the words of Paul Harvey, you need to hear "the rest of the story." In the midst of Naomi's bitterness, God gave hints of hope, of life. First, food became plentiful again in Bethlehem, so Naomi made up her mind to return home. Then, Ruth, one of Naomi's daughters-in-law determined to stick to Naomi like a daughter. As several weeks and months pass, the story centers around a man named Boaz, one kin to Naomi. He is a kinsman, and if he is willing, he can be the kinsman-redeemer of Ruth, Naomi, and all their possessions. This decision wasn't an easy one, for the misfortunes of Naomi and Ruth (in addition to losing her husband, she was a foreigner, and an enemy Moabitess at that!) signaled to others that they were cursed by God. These women were outcasts. If Boaz would act as their redeemer, he would have to be willing to become a curse. And yet he redeems them by purchasing them! Instead of receiving a curse, Boaz gets blessed, for he has a son who becomes the grandfather of King David. The LORD turned Naomi's hopelessness into hope-filled-ness. She went from death to life. She went from utter poverty to a family of royalty!

And don't forget Ruth, a one-time enemy of God and false worshipper. She became a child of Yahweh, the One True God. The LORD even included her in the "Who's Who" ancestral line of King David. These ladies were outcasts no longer!

God is faithful in watching over His own. He gave Naomi a promise of life in the person of her kinsman-redeemer. Boaz was no mere figure in history. His family became the most important family in Israel for from him came the King.

> But why cause such a fuss about this line
> Of David, and bitter lives—yours or mine?
> And a Redeemer who buys to b'come a curse?
> Good questions, dear friend, please read the next verse.

Application Idea
Travel to a local hardware store and buy a large nail (several inches long). You will also need either a drill or a hot glue gun and a few inches of red ribbon (9" should be enough). Drill a hole in the nail to thread a piece of ribbon through it or hot glue the ribbon to the nail. Hang the nail on your Christmas tree close to the trunk. You may want to include a small paper tag on the ribbon with these words:

Christmas Nail—the true joy of a Christmas tree comes only because of the pain of a cursed tree to which Jesus was nailed in order to redeem us from the curse of the law (cf. Galatians 3:3).

"Angels We Have Heard on High"
Origin: Traditional French Carol, 18th century

Angels we have heard on high
Sweetly singing o'er the plains,
And the mountains in reply
Echoing their joyous strains.

Refrain:
Gloria, in excelsis Deo!
Gloria, in excelsis Deo!

Shepherds, why this jubilee?
Why your joyous strains prolong?
What the gladsome tidings be
Which inspire your heavenly song?

Come to Bethlehem and see
Christ Whose birth the angels sing;
Come, adore on bended knee,
Christ the Lord, the newborn King.

See Him in a manger laid,
Whom the choirs of angels praise;
Mary, Joseph, lend your aid,
While our hearts in love we raise.

Prayer

Father God, thank You for taking an outcast like me and including me in Your family through faith in Your Son, the Lord Jesus Christ. He is my Redeemer and King and I pray in His name, Amen.

December 13   A Kingdom for All Eternity

"I will raise up your offspring after you, who shall come from your body, and I will establish his kingdom... I will establish the throne of his kingdom forever. I will be to him a father, and he shall be to me a son.... And your house and your kingdom shall be made sure forever before me. Your throne shall be established forever."(2 Samuel 7:12, 13b-14a, 16)

Imagine being David, King of Israel 3,000 years ago. By the hand of Almighty God, you have experienced tremendous victories over surrounding enemies. A few years earlier, the Lord preserved your life from the evil intention of King Saul to kill you. Furthermore, the ark of the covenant of Yahweh, the One True God, has come to rest in the capital city of Jerusalem. God has given you life and personal achievements, and the sign of His presence now sits within your midst.

How would you feel? Grateful? Yes. Humbled? Without a doubt. Determined to do something in return? Absolutely! So, like David, you begin to think about your surroundings—extremely nice house, servants at your beck and call, high tech security from any and every enemy. But then you realize that the ark of God has but a tent for a dwelling place, hardly a place of dignity. So you decide to build a temple for the Lord, a beautiful, lasting edifice for your Sovereign. Now that's a noble and honorable response, don't you think?

Except for the word of God, we would all be applauding such a lofty ideal. God responds, however, through the voice of Nathan the prophet, saying He is not restricted by any one particular place. His ark has sat inside a tent for hundreds of years because He is a God-Who-Moves. He desires to speak to and act through His people as they move together throughout the land.

On the other hand, God is worthy of our very best, and so an elaborate temple could house His covenant promises. David would not be allowed to build it, because of all the bloodshed during his days. So God promises that David's son—whose reign shall be marked by peace rather than war—shall build Him such a palace.

Here's where the promise results in goose-bumps. Not only does the Lord promise David a son to carry on his family name (all children are precious gifts from God, but the vast majority of men take pride in their family name, a name that lives on through their sons), but He also claims uniqueness for one of David's descendants. First, this Davidic son would also be God's Son. Over the next several generations, the Jews began to associate the title "Son of David" with the Son of God, also known as the Messiah, the Christ of God.

Furthermore, this one would establish an eternal kingdom, something the world has never known. All of the world's great leaders and nations both before and after David have risen and fallen, never lasting more than a few hundred years at best. Even the great nations of today have existed under their current constitutional make-up a very short time. The Son of David, however, will reign forever. The only way He could reign forever is if He lives forever. So that means He either never dies or He comes back from the dead, never to die again. Rising from the dead is exactly what Jesus of Nazareth has done and since He conquered death, He will never die again. Jesus is the Son of David!

> Has this Davidic Son, the Christ, already come
> And about His appointed work, has it been done?
> And does He now sit upon His eternal throne
> And reign over a people all His very own?
> Or must we still patiently to the future look?
> No! For Christ has come to earth! It is in God's Book!

Application Idea

Get online and search for a few major world leaders (Ramses II, Alexander the Great, Napoleon, Hitler, Churchill, Washington, Lincoln, Stalin, etc.). Notice their birthdates and death dates. Are any still alive? How long did they live? What did their people think of them? In what ways is Jesus greater than these world leaders?

"The First Noel"
Origin: Traditional English Carol, 18th century

> The first Noel the angel did say,
> Was to certain poor shepherds in fields as they lay;
> In fields where they lay keeping their sheep,
> On a cold winter's night that was so deep.

Refrain:
Noel, Noel, Noel, Noel,
Born is the King of Israel.

For all to see there was a star
Shining in the east, beyond them far;
And to the earth it gave great light,
And so it continued both day and night.

And by the light of that same star
The wise men came from country far;
To seek for a King was their intent,
And to follow the star wherever it went.

Then let us all with one accord
Sing praises to our heavenly Lord
Who hath made heav'n and earth of naught,
And with His blood mankind hath bought.

Prayer

Your reign, O Lord, is eternal and universal. We express our gratitude for Your personal rule in our lives. Help us live as obedient subjects to You. In Jesus' name, Amen.

December 14   **He Is Wonderful Counselor**

For to us a child is born, to us a son is given, and the government shall be upon his shoulder, and his name shall be called Wonderful Counselor... (Isaiah 9:6)

Poll average Christians about their favorite Christmas song sung in churches and Handel's "Messiah"is sure to rank toward the top. Composed in 1741, it gained popularity within a few short years. While taken from a number of biblical texts, Isaiah 9:6 is one of the most prominent passages in the song, from the KJV: "For unto us a Child is born, unto us a Son is given; and the government shall be upon his shoulders..." Over the next few days, I want to look at different facets of Isaiah 9:6-7 and the expectations of its coming Ruler.

One interesting observation of these opening words is how God reveals this coming One to Isaiah—He speaks in the perfect tense, something which occurred in the past with present ramifications (is born, is given). But the past tense is not intended, for who, prior to Isaiah, fulfilled these characteristics and expectations? No one. Thus, God speaks of a future event, but conveys it in the past, as though it is a settled event—nothing would undo what the Lord had planned to do.

Also, the fact that "to us a child is born" clearly points to the humanity of the coming Ruler. This Ruler isn't merely a child but a Son, one dignified to accept His royal lineage as Israel's hope. This Son will be "given" to us. The question arises, "will be given by whom?" The passive voice in Scripture often implies that God will do the action, what scholars call the theological passive. If this notion is correct here, the Son will be given to us by God. Jesus probably had this passage in mind when He said, "For God so loved the world, that he gave his only Son..." (John 3:16).

Isaiah provides a four-fold name or title of this Son, beginning with Wonderful Counselor. Your initial thought may be "Wait, He is Wonderful *and* Counselor—those are two names!" Well, that certainly is how Handel's "Messiah" portrays Him, but each of the other titles occurs in pairs, what we might call an adjective and a noun (Mighty God, Eternal Father, Peacely Prince—see below). Thus, Wonderful Counselor goes together with the notion of "a Wonder of a Counselor." His counsel would be far greater than the counsel of man, for it is wonderful, marvelous, and even extraordinary. This term describes the miracles of God done in Egypt, such as the ten plagues, the parting of the Red Sea, the guidance by pillar of cloud and fire, the provisions of food and water in the wilderness and the like (cf. Psalm 78:12-16)—these things were wonderful, marvelous works of our God!

How many times have you discovered the counsel of men and women to fall short of what you really needed? The Messiah's counsel will always be wonderful. Later in his book, Isaiah observes how Yahweh of Hosts "is wonderful in counsel and excellent in wisdom" (28:29). The pairing of Yahweh's wonderful advice and Christ as a Wonderful Counselor go arm-in-arm: like Father, like Son.

No one instructs and counsels like the Lord Himself. This understanding caused the Apostle Paul to write of Christ: "In whom are hidden all the treasures of wisdom and knowledge" (Colossians 2:3). That God would promise to give us a Son who would be a Wonderful Counselor is truly marvelous!

> A hopeless world does result in many shed tears,
> But strange things are now coming upon my own ears:
> A Wonderful Counselor who gives great advice,
> Only Messiah Himself could be so precise.

Application Idea

Make a list of the wonderful things the Lord has done for you. If multiple family members take part in this project, you may want them to take turns writing down his/her blessings. Write them on a poster to put on the wall or on a piece of construction paper to place on the refrigerator. Keep this reminder up through the Christmas season to help you remember how wonderful Christ is.

"Messiah" (excerpt)
Author: George Frideric Handel, 1741

> For unto us a Child is born,
> Unto us a Son is given,
> And the government shall be upon His shoulder:
> And His name shall be called Wonderful, Counsellor,
> the mighty God, the everlasting Father, the Prince of Peace.

Prayer

Lord God, You know just what we need: You sent Jesus to be our Wonderful Counselor and give us the guidance we need in life. Thank You for being so good to us. We pray in Jesus' name, Amen.

December 15   **He Is Mighty God**

... and the government shall be upon his shoulder, and his name shall be called Wonderful Counselor, Mighty God... (Isaiah 9:6)

Have you ever tried to compare apples to oranges? I doubt it, because they are different fruits and while people often compare apples to apples or oranges to oranges, no one compares them to each other. I've had more than my fair share of conversations with Jehovah's Witnesses about the full deity of Jesus Christ. On several occasions, one of them will say something like "Christ is never called 'Almighty' God, but only 'Mighty' God." But that's like comparing apples to oranges. I'll tell you why.

I'll ask for forgiveness up front in referencing a couple of Hebrew titles. I don't mean to sound smart or speak over your head. I think you'll pick it up well. The Hebrew phrase "Mighty God" is *El Gibbor*. This phrase is not inferior to "Almighty God," which is *El Shaddai*. The two terms for "mighty" (*gibbor*) and "almighty" (*shaddai*) are different, unrelated Hebrew terms. It is similar to our English use of the words "brilliant" and "strong." While certain contexts may use either word, they are not typical synonyms. Comparing *gibbor* and *shaddai* is apples and oranges.

Okay, but how is *El Gibbor* (Mighty God) a reference to the full deity of Jesus Christ? It just so happens the Scriptures call Yahweh "Mighty God" (*El Gibbor*) elsewhere, as seen below:

➤ For the LORD your God is God of gods and Lord of lords, the great, the mighty (*gibbor*), and the awesome God (*El*), who is not partial and takes no bribe (Deuteronomy 10:17)

➤ In that day the remnant of Israel and the survivors of the house of Jacob will no more lean on him who struck them, but will lean on the LORD, the Holy One of Israel, in truth. A remnant will return, the remnant of Jacob, to the mighty God (*El Gibbor*) (Isaiah 10:20-21)

➤ Ah, Lord GOD! It is you who have made the heavens and the earth by your great power and by your outstretched arm! Nothing is too hard for you. You show steadfast love to thousands, but you repay the guilt of fathers to their children after them, O great and mighty God (*El Gibbor*), whose name is the LORD of hosts, great in counsel and mighty in deed... (Jeremiah 32:17-19a)

The fact that Yahweh is the Mighty God raises the understanding of Isaiah's coming Ruler, who is also called the Mighty God. As a matter of fact, Isaiah only uses *El* for God, never for a lesser being (like an angel or a king). Thus, the Mighty God to come has the power to execute divine plans.

One more observation is in order: mighty (*gibbor*) can also mean "hero," as in the LORD is a Heroic God. You may be familiar with Bonnie Tyler's song "I Need a Hero" or maybe you have watched *The Avengers* or movies about Batman, Spiderman, Superman or X-Men. Do you know what these heroes and superheroes always do? They come to the rescue of those in need and they are right on time. That analogy is appropriate for our Messiah: the Mighty/Heroic God who rescues sinners and does so in a timely manner.

So Yahweh is Mighty/Heroic God. The same is true for Messiah. That sounds like the Messiah is fully God. So let's quit messing around with apples and oranges and serve Him. We'll find Him to be the Hero we really need.

> Now let the following statement be like an oath:
> Our great God, He is Almighty and Mighty, both
> And all other superheroes He does exceed,
> Jesus Christ is the Hero we all truly need.

Application Idea

Who's your favorite superhero? Why? How is Jesus like that superhero? What other superhero qualities does Jesus possess? If you have kids, let them dress up as a superhero (putting on masks or wearing a towel for a cape). Ask them what superhero powers they would like to have and explain how Jesus is even greater.

"Thou Didst Leave Thy Throne"
Author: Emily E.S. Elliott, 1864

> Thou didst leave Thy throne and Thy kingly crown,
> When Thou camest to earth for me;
> But in Bethlehem's home was there found no room
> For Thy holy nativity.

Refrain:
O come to my heart, Lord Jesus,
There is room in my heart for Thee!

Heaven's arches rang when the angels sang,
Proclaiming Thy royal degree;
But of lowly birth didst Thou come to earth,
And in great humility.

The foxes found rest, and the birds their nest
In the shade of the forest tree;
But Thy couch was the sod, O Thou Son of God,
In the deserts of Galilee.

Thou camest, O Lord, with the living Word,
That should set Thy people free;
But with mocking scorn and with crown of thorn,
They bore Thee to Calvary.

When the heavens shall ring and the angels sing
At Thy coming to victory,
Let Thy voice call me home, saying "Yet there is room,
There is room at My side for thee."

My heart shall rejoice, Lord Jesus,
When Thou comest and callest for me!

Prayer

Lord, thank You for Your word and what it teaches us about the nature and full deity of Christ. We know He is heaven's Hero, sent to rescue us from sin. Help us cling to Him in hope, for we pray in His name, Amen.

December 16   He Is Eternal Father

... and the government shall be upon his shoulder, and his name shall be called Wonderful Counselor, Mighty God, Everlasting Father... (Isaiah 9:6)

When you think of your father, what comes to mind? Unfortunately for far too many people today, few positives stand out. Some fathers are away in service to their country. Other dads have failed their children in their fatherly responsibilities. Father's Day doesn't get near the hoopla Mother's Day gets.

So what qualities should a father have? He should demonstrate love, discipline, protection, provision, care, comfort, loyalty, leadership, support, instruction and more. A father should challenge his children to become better at whatever they do. He should fix broken things around the house for his kids, and if he doesn't know how to fix them, he should negotiate a fair deal in its repair.

Now think about Christ. One scholar has stated there are more than 250 titles for the Messiah from Genesis to Revelation. Each title underscores a different facet of His being. Of all these titles, one of the most interesting to me is Everlasting Father. Other English translations say the Eternal Father, but the idea is the same—He is the Father of eternity.

Let me make something immediately clear: Jesus Christ, the second Person of the Trinity, is not the same as God the Father. The Father and the Son are two distinct Persons within the Godhead. So what does Isaiah mean when he refers to the Messiah as Everlasting Father? He probably intends to convey the Jewish notion of "source" or "originator." Jesus said of Satan: "When he tells a lie, he speaks from his own nature, because he is a liar and the father of liars" (John 8:44). Jesus says all lies originate with the devil; he is the source of every falsehood.

With this comprehension of father as "source" or "originator," you can see what Isaiah means with Everlasting Father as a title for the Messiah. Christ will do for His own for an eternity what an earthly father would do for his children for as long as he lived. Just as an earthly father can love and provide and care for his family, so Christ will provide and comfort and protect His family for all eternity. As a father sacrifices for his children, so Christ sacrificed Himself.

One more thing: don't overlook the significance of Christ as an *Everlasting* Father. Following David's reign, kings in Israel and Judah came and went. While some were good kings, many were evil kings. No matter their character, however, *none* brought permanent stability to the kingdom. Any good deed could be undone by a future monarch. All of that stops with Christ as the Everlasting Father. Everything He sets in place will not change, at least not for all eternity.

> So ever more clearly I'm beginning to see
> Jesus Christ as the Father of Eternity,
> As provider, protector, instructor and more,
> 'Twill be amazing to see all He has in store.

Application Idea

What's something special your father (or grandfather, if your dad wasn't in the picture) gave to you or did with you? What made it so special? What are some things the Lord has done for you that are similar to what your father has done?

"God Rest Ye Merry Gentlemen"
Origin: Traditional English Carol, c. 1760

> God rest ye merry, gentlemen,
> Let nothing you dismay,
> For Jesus Christ, our Saviour,
> Was born upon this day
> To save us all from Satan's power
> When we were gone astray.

> Refrain:
> O tidings of comfort and joy,
> comfort and joy;
> O tidings of comfort and joy!

> In Bethlehem in Jewry
> This blessed Babe was born,
> And laid within a manger
> Upon this blessed morn;

The which his mother Mary
Nothing did take in scorn.

From God our heavenly Father
A blessed angel came,
And unto certain shepherds
Brought tidings of the same,
How that in Bethlehem was born
The Son of God by name.

'Fear not,' then said the angel,
'Let nothing you affright;
This day is born a Saviour
Of virtue, power and might,
So frequently to vanquish all
The friends of Satan quite.'

The shepherds at these tidings
Rejoiced much in mind,
And left their flocks a-feeding
In tempest, storm and wind,
And went to Bethlehem straightway
This blessed Babe to find.

But when to Bethlehem they came,
Whereat this Infant lay,
They found him in a manger
Where oxen fed on hay;
His mother Mary, kneeling,
Unto the Lord did pray.

Now to the Lord sing praises,
All you within this place,
And with true love and brotherhood
Each other now embrace.
The holy tide of Christmas
All others doth efface.

Prayer

Lord Jesus, thank You for being like a father in all the ways You have provided for us. Thank You also for teaching us and being there for us. We love You and thank You for these things in Your name, Amen.

December 17   **He Is Prince of Peace**

... and the government shall be upon his shoulder, and his name shall be called Wonderful Counselor, Mighty God, Everlasting Father, Prince of Peace. Of the increase of his government and of peace there will be no end, on the throne of David and over his kingdom, to establish it and uphold it with justice and with righteousness from this time forth and forevermore. (Isaiah 9:6-7)

Have you ever experienced peace in your home? Parents of small children have all but forgotten what peace is. Moms and Dads look for places to escape to get some "peace and quiet." Husbands and wives may leave their house for a few hours to get away from the constant arguing and get some "peace." Is it any wonder peace is so hard to find in the home when nations all around the world— from the Middle East to the Far East to Latin America to Africa and the UN—fail at bringing peace to conflicts? Whether we turn on the news or try to de-stress by watching Hollywood's movie stars (hardly the models of stable homes), we don't have many good examples before us. What the world needs corporately and what we need individually is peace.

As Isaiah wraps up his titles for the Messiah, he calls Him the "Prince of Peace." Peace (*shalom*) saturates the pages of Scripture. It communicates harmony, wholeness and well-being. The Jews said "Shalom" both as a greeting (cf. Isaiah 57:19) and in bidding farewell (cf. Exodus 4:18), more than a standard "hello" and "goodbye," but as a blessing—"may God bring you peace" or "may the Lord keep you in peace."

The Messiah as Prince of Peace means He administers well-being to others. As prince, He governs and gives others peace with God when they trust Him (cf. Romans 5:1). He also grants the peace of God, the harmony God brings to a person who trusts in Him (cf. Philippians 4:7).

Ultimately, peace defines this Prince's rule and government. The "government... upon his shoulder" means Christ is able to bear the burden of His people. His reign of peace will result in prosperity for His people. Success would have been important in Isaiah's day, with enemies mounted all around Israel, and how much more important is it in our own day? The Messiah's kingdom of peace will be founded "with justice and with righteousness from this time forth and forevermore." Although the justice system of this world is corrupt and full of holes, the government to come will not only right every wrong, but it will last for all eternity.

First-century Palestine desperately needed a reminder of peace, as the Jewish people struggled under Roman rule. At the birth of Jesus, the heavenly host sang: "Glory to God in the highest, and on earth peace among those with whom he is pleased!" (Luke 2:14). The people of the earth need peace and peace is what our good God delivered in sending the Messiah.

> For unto us a Child has been already born,
> He came long ago, on what we call Christmas morn,
> And unto us a Son has surely been given,
> He's God's perfect, precious Gift sent down from heaven.
> And the government sits upon His shoulders strong,
> He's worthy of our highest praise and our best song:
> Wonderful Counselor and Mighty God is He,
> Prince of Peace, even Father of Eternity!

Application Idea

What is something which helps put you at peace? Cuddly animals, ice cream, music, chocolate? Visit a pet store and stroke the back of a dog or cat or go to a restaurant for chocolate (or ice cream) or simply curl up on the couch and listen to some soothing music. How is the peace Jesus offers like that thing which puts you at peace?

"Comfort, Comfort Ye My People"
Author: Johannes G. Olearius, 1671;
Translator: Catherine Winkworth, 1863

> Comfort, comfort ye My people,
> Speak ye peace, thus saith our God;
> Comfort those who sit in darkness,
> Mourning 'neath their sorrow's load;
> Speak ye to Jerusalem
> Of the peace that waits for them;
> Tell her that her sins I cover,
> And her warfare now is over.

For the herald's voice is crying
In the desert far and near,
Bidding all men to repentance,
Since the kingdom now is here.
O that warning cry obey!
Now prepare for God a way!
Let the valleys rise to meet Him,
And the hills bow down to greet Him.

Yea, her sins our God will pardon,
Blotting out each dark misdeed;
All that well deserved His anger
He will no more see nor heed.
She has suffered many a day,
Now her griefs have passed away,
God will change her pining sadness
Into ever springing gladness.

Make ye straight what long was crooked,
Make the rougher places plain:
Let your hearts be true and humble,
As befits His holy reign,
For the glory of the Lord
Now o'er the earth is shed abroad,
And all flesh shall see the token
That His Word is never broken.

Prayer

We lift You up, good and glorious Father, for You have set us at
peace with You through Your Son, the Lord Jesus Christ. Help us
experience that peace as we continually trust You and the
completed work of Christ on the cross for our sins. We ask these
things in Jesus' name, Amen.

December 18   He Is the Branch of Hope in the Tree Stump

There shall forth a shoot from the stump of Jesse, and a branch from his roots shall bear fruit.... In that day the root of Jesse shall stand as a signal for the peoples—of him shall the nations inquire, and his resting place shall be glorious. (Isaiah 11:1, 10)

Tree stumps can be a bit of a nuisance. No longer does the tree provide shade or beauty to behold. All which remains is a stump. And if the stump is in your yard, you have to mow around it. For extra money and energy, you can remove a stump and that's what many people do. Why leave a stump? What's it going to do, grow again? Maybe.

The Jewish people in Isaiah's day were losing hope. Surrounding nations were fighting with them and threatening to overthrow them. Over the next several decades, Assyria and Babylonia would take them captive, laying waste of their homeland. Many who picked up Isaiah's scroll were looking for notes of hope. They would not be disappointed.

Isaiah reminds us that Jesse, David's father, would see his line revive. Though the line of Davidic kings would come to an end, just like a stump is the end of a tree, One branch among the roots would be productive. Later prophets picked up on this fruit-bearing branch the way Isaiah intended: as Messianic hope. Speaking about the kingdoms of Israel and Judah, Jeremiah commented, "In those days and at that time I will cause a righteous Branch to spring up for David, and he shall execute justice and righteousness in the land" (33:15; cf. 23:5). Zechariah, too, spoke of one to come called the Branch, bringing hope to God's people (cf. 3:8; 6:12).

During the first-century, Matthew possibly had these texts in mind when he wrote of Jesus, "And he went and lived in a city called Nazareth, that what was spoken by the prophet might be fulfilled: 'He shall be called a Nazarene'" (2:23). This verse has mystified scholars, for no Old Testament passage says "He shall be called a Nazarene."

But maybe we need to look closer. Hebrew is a consonant-only alphabet; there are no vowels. Scribes added vowel pointings (markings) centuries later to help readers with pronunciation. The Hebrew word for branch is transliterated as *nzr*, the same root for the word Nazareth (minus the ending). When Matthew sees prophetic fulfillment in Nazareth, maybe he is thinking about the Branch (*nzr*) of hope.

By the way, even Isaiah had already been given a glimpse into God's hope for His people. At his commissioning, God spoke of a surviving remnant through the times of desolation: "'Like a terebinth or an oak, whose stump remains when it is felled.' The holy seed is its stump" (6:13). The stump refers not just to God's people, but a singular Seed, One who is holy Himself and from the tree of Jesse and line of David. His appearance will bring hope not only for Israel but for all the nations, as they seek Him to find rest. The good news is Jesus is the "holy seed" and "Root of David" who is victorious (cf. Revelation 5:5)!

Did you know that even though you may cut down a tree, there sometimes remains a hidden vigor in it, allowing it to sprout again? Such a thing can happen with a black locust tree. So it is with God's people. Just when things appear dead and hopeless, God brings life out of a little, from His Righteous Branch Jesus.

Isaiah's hope lied in Jesse's very own Root,
A Branch from a tree stump that would produce much fruit.
His life revealed He is the Seed of holiness
We know Him well, for He's none other than Jesus!

Application Idea

Create (or borrow) a fun Christmas tradition with your family. As a suggestion, hide a single ornament in your Christmas tree and let children compete to see who can find it first (we use the so-called German Christmas Pickle Ornament). Offer an extra present or treat to the winner (my wife and I have found it works better each year to exempt the previous year's winner from winning two years in a roar, but we encourage him/her to help the others). How does the symbol of the Christmas tree bring hope? How is Jesus like a branch?

"O Holy Night!"
Author: Placide Cappeau, 1847;
Translator: John S. Dwight, 1855

O holy night, the stars are brightly shining;
It is the night of the dear Savior's birth!
Long lay the world in sin and error pining,
Till He appeared and the soul felt its worth.
A thrill of hope, the weary soul rejoices,
For yonder breaks a new and glorious morn.
Fall on your knees, O hear the angel voices!
O night divine, O night when Christ was born!
O night, O holy night, O night divine!

Led by the light of faith serenely beaming,
With glowing hearts by His cradle we stand.
So led by light of a star sweetly gleaming,
Here came the wise men from Orient land.
The King of kings lay thus in lowly manger,
In all our trials born to be our Friend!
He knows our need—to our weakness is no stranger.
Behold your King; before Him lowly bend!
Behold your King; before Him lowly bend!

Truly He taught us to love one another;
His law is love and His Gospel is peace.
Chains shall He break for the slave is our brother
And in His Name all oppression shall cease.
Sweet hymns of joy in grateful chorus raise we,
Let all within us praise His holy Name!
Christ is the Lord! O praise His name forever!
His power and glory evermore proclaim!
His power and glory evermore proclaim!

Prayer
Dear Jesus, we praise You for being a strong, righteous Branch and
Giver of hope to us. Help us find strength in You. We pray in
Your holy name, Amen.

December 19   **Upon Him Rests the Spirit of the LORD**

And the Spirit of the LORD shall rest upon him, the Spirit of wisdom and understanding, the Spirit of counsel and might, the Spirit of knowledge and the fear of the LORD. And his delight shall be in the fear of the LORD. (Isaiah 11:2-3a)

Have you ever watched a strongest-man contest? The men compete in various events with emphases on the strength of their arms, legs, back or shoulders. Or maybe you have observed a beauty pageant with ladies contending with their looks, talent and knowledge. No one wins a beauty contest on good looks alone and no man is deemed the strongest simply because he has big arms. Winners of these competitions possess multiple favorable attributes.

The world's need for a Savior is not to be met with a single characteristic, but a multi-faceted individual. The stirring speeches of Hitler or the military genius of Napoleon or the sheer size of the army of Alexander the Great would never be enough to demand the world's allegiance. What the world needs is a Leader who is wise, knowledgeable and strong. Such a Deliverer must also set a worthy example for others to follow (unlike most world leaders of the past).

Isaiah's message of the restored Davidic line through the Messiah fulfills and exceeds these descriptions and is just what the world needs. When reading the passage above, you cannot help but note the seven-fold elaboration of the divine endowment of the Messianic King. Beginning with the Spirit of the LORD resting on Him (see the Spirit's descent on Jesus at His baptism, Matthew 3:16-17), which refers to the Messiah's anointing, the other six characteristics occur in three pairs.

First, see Christ's intellectual, or ruling, abilities. He will possess wisdom, knowing what is right and doing it. His understanding is the ability to see the heart of the issue. Jesus fulfilled this description for He "increased in wisdom and in stature and in favor with God and man" (Luke 2:52) and "he himself knew what was in man" (John 2:25).

Second, the Messiah has practical skills. The Spirit of counsel is both a general capacity to have a right judgment in all things and the ability to devise a right course of action. His power refers to

His ability to see the course of action through. Others viewed Jesus as "a prophet mighty in deed and word before God and all the people" (Luke 24:19). He was mighty in His counsel (cf. Isaiah 9:6).

Finally, this anointed Leader demonstrates spiritual qualities. He has knowledge, not so much of knowing *things* (as wisdom and understanding address) but knowing *people*. The word for knowledge comes from the verb "to know" and refers to enjoying a personal, intimate relationship with others (cf. Genesis 4:1; 1 Samuel 2:12; Amos 3:2). The last attribute, fear of the LORD, is the proper foundation for knowledge (Proverbs 1:7). It includes moral concern, obedience, loyalty and sincere desire to worship God. Fear of the LORD occurs in contexts of sacrifices and worship, where worshippers approach God in the temple with a sacrifice for their sins. They approach in fear, for they revere Yahweh, and don't want to offer an unpleasing sacrifice. But the ultimate act is not of being afraid but of worship and awe (Psalms 33:8, 18; 67:7; 130:4). Again, Jesus knew people intimately and He knew and pleased God the Father with His life of worship (Matthew 11:27) and it was a "delight" for our Lord to live this way!

Therefore, when you think about Jesus, consider how He is a beautiful Savior and how He delivers with a strong arm, but don't stop at those things. He is so much more, for He is complete and perfect in His attributes. He blows away all other competition.

The role of both Father and Spirit in the Son
Proved to ev'ryone He could never be outdone.
So get ready and let all the land's church bells ring
Announcing the coming of our great God and King!

Application Idea

Take a few minutes to talk about each other's positive qualities. What is it you like about others in your family? Share why you appreciate those things. What are some qualities you love about Jesus? Why?

"Come, Thou Long-Expected Jesus"
Author: Charles Wesley, 1745

Come, Thou long expected Jesus
Born to set Thy people free;
From our fears and sins release us,
Let us find our rest in Thee.
Israel's Strength and Consolation,
Hope of all the earth Thou art;
Dear Desire of every nation,
Joy of every longing heart.

Born Thy people to deliver,
Born a child and yet a King,
Born to reign in us forever,
Now Thy gracious kingdom bring.
By Thine own eternal Spirit
Rule in all our hearts alone;
By Thine all sufficient merit,
Raise us to Thy glorious throne.

Prayer

O Father, You have demonstrated Your perfect wisdom in sending
Christ at just the right time and You anointed Him with Your Spirit
to demonstrate He is the Messiah. We praise You for these things
in Jesus' name, Amen.

JOEL BREIDENBAUGH

FULFILLMENT OF THE PROMISE

JOEL BREIDENBAUGH

December 20   **The Promise Fulfilled**

And the angel answered her, "The Holy Spirit will come upon you, and the power of the Most High will overshadow you; therefore the child to be born will be called holy—the Son of God." (Luke 1:35)

The Promise. Lots of angles, but the same promise. Ever since sin entered the world in Genesis 3, God promised victory over Satan for the Seed of Eve. He promised blessing and hope surrounding the Seed of Abraham. The Lord sounded and hinted at a promise of life to Naomi and His people through a Kinsman-Redeemer— one greater than Boaz. He promised to rule and reign and bring His people peace, as One who transcends history yet intervenes as royalty. Unlike us, God *keeps every promise* that He *makes*.

When God sent the angel Gabriel to the town of Nazareth to a virgin woman named Mary 2,000 years ago, it is safe to say that few were thinking about His promise. Now we might consider the likes of Simeon or Anna (Luke 2), but those genuinely longing for the Promise were few. Too many people in 1st-century Palestine were amazed and caught off-guard by the work of Jesus. They hadn't necessarily forgotten the Promise. They just weren't looking for its fulfillment. At that time. In that way. Yet God kept the promise He had made. The One whose origins were from of old would step into the womb of Mary.

We know the story. Jesus was born of a virgin. The angel Gabriel announced Christ's coming to Mary, explaining to her how she would conceive Jesus though she was a virgin—God would cause it to happen. Jesus would be the "holy" One, and the human authors of Scripture declare in unison: Jesus lived a sinless life.

But there's more. He was the greatest Teacher. He was an extraordinary miracle-Worker. He was none other than God in human flesh. In His deity, He could offer a perfect life to satisfy God's wrath, a life with an eternal nature that could be a once-for-all sacrifice for sin. In His humanity, He could stand in the place of mankind as our substitute for sin. He could represent God for us. He could represent us to God. Not only would Jesus die, but He would rise from the dead to prove that He is the long-awaited Messiah, the Suffering Servant who has risen to reign. He is the Lord, the very Son of God. Only those who turn from their sin and trust in Him are declared right with God. That's His perfect *promise*.

It is no surprise for most of us that this story has pointed to Jesus. We've heard the message enough that we can connect the dots before they are even put in place. Where's the mystery in this piece of history?

It's in the promise. Better yet, it's in the Promise-Maker and Promise-Keeper—the Lord Himself. Who can immediately promise victory in a moment of defeat and clarify that promise over centuries to come so that its fulfillment would be seen by both the simple and the wise? God. He's in control and He's worth trusting and He's worth living for every moment. But don't take my word for it. After all, it's God's promise.

Promises can be made, promises can be broken,
Promises that are kept are more than just a token.
Promises of God are specific and crystal-clear
God's answer for human sin has already come near
Who is the Seed of Eve and the Seed of Abraham?
And who is the hope of every woman and man?
Who is our kinsman-Redeemer and Ancient of Days?
None other than Jesus, the Son of God we must praise!
When you read the Holy Scripture, do not be amiss
At the plan of God, who fulfills every promise.

Application Idea

Bake a family treat (cookies, pie, etc.). Let the kids participate in its preparation. Once it comes out of the oven, let everyone get a good whiff of the aroma. Now that the expectations are heightened, let them eat some of it. How did you like waiting on the finished product? Did the smell get you excited? Did the taste exceed your anticipation? How satisfying is the fulfillment of great hope? How happy do you think people were 2,000 years ago when the Messiah came to them?

"What Child Is This"
Author: William C. Dix, 1865

What Child is this who, laid to rest
On Mary's lap is sleeping?
Whom angels greet with anthems sweet,
While shepherds watch are keeping?

Refrain:
This, this is Christ the King,
Whom shepherds guard and angels sing:
Haste, haste, to bring Him laud,
The Babe, the Son of Mary.

Why lies He in such mean estate,
Where ox and ass are feeding?
Good Christians, fear, for sinners here
The silent Word is pleading.

So bring Him incense, gold and myrrh,
Come peasant, king to own Him;
The King of kings salvation brings;
Let loving hearts enthrone Him.

Prayer

Father, thank You for fulfilling Your promise in sending Jesus into the world as the long-awaited Messiah. Help us wait on You to fulfill Your promise to send Jesus a second time to finalize our redemption. In Jesus' name we pray, Amen.

December 21   **Angelic News of Joy**

And the angel said to them, "Fear not, for behold, I bring you good news of great joy that will be for all the people. For unto you is born this day in the city of David a Savior, who is Christ the Lord. And this will be a sign for you: you will find a baby wrapped in swaddling cloths and lying in a manger."
(Luke 2:10-12)

Have you ever seen an angel? If you are a grandparent, I'm not talking about your grandkids; neither am I speaking of meeting a female named, "Angel." I mean a real, bona fide angel. We've all witnessed artistic expressions of angels with long air, large wings, and a certain aura about them. Many people these days have cited angelic encounters, but most of them seem hard to believe. I think it is fair to say that angelic appearances are far from the norm. Angels don't make appearances very often. But when they do, watch out! When we read stories containing angels in the Bible, the observers always display fear (which explains why most so-called angel-sightings today aren't true—the "fear factor" is missing from the accounts).

Just over 2,000 years ago, an angel of the Lord appeared to some shepherds stationed in the country outside of Bethlehem. The angel had come to deliver a message. In fact, the word "angel" literally means "messenger," and though angels may be intimidating and protective, one of their primary responsibilities is speaking a message from God. The initial greeting, "Fear not, for behold," intends to set the recipients at ease while getting their attention to hear what follows. The message is exceedingly great news for everyone. Had you and I been there, the angel would undoubtedly have our complete attention.

The angel then explains his statement of joyful news: that very day in Bethlehem (the city of David) a Savior had been born. "Savior" is one who saves/delivers. Though it can mean physical deliverance from an enemy, it also conveys spiritual deliverance or salvation. Such a description was not attributed to any average Joe.

The message says this Savior "is Christ the Lord!" Christ refers to the Messiah, the One God promised from old to give His people hope, comfort, and ultimate deliverance. The Jews understood the Christ to be the "Son of David." Matthew records how the Pharisees, a group of Jewish leaders long ago, agreed the

Christ would be the "son of David" (22:41-42). Jews believed the promise made to David about a future son (2 Samuel 7) would be none other than their Christ, the one who defends and delivers God's people.

In addition to this, Christ became associated with the title "Lord," meaning master, ruler. This term is highly significant, for it is used for God throughout the Bible. The same Jews who believed Christ would be the Son of David also understood Christ to be Lord (see Psalm 110:1 in light of Matthew 22:41-45). Therefore, the Christ is a Savior/Deliverer and the Son of David, as well as the Lord, God—who transcends time—stepping into our world of time and space.

Finally, the angel added a sign to confirm the validity of his message: find the baby wrapped up and lying in a manger. A newborn wrapped snuggly was quite common, and it's still done today. Finding this baby in a feeding trough, a manger, among animals, would be a rare find indeed, full of humility.

But news like this alone, though great as it may be
Is not nearly the same as having eyes that clearly see
To confirm this good news of great, glad joy is true
Changing the lives eternally of me and you.

Application Idea

Look at some family photos which bring you much joy—a wedding, births of children/grandchildren, special events. What is it about those pictures that cause you to have such joy? What was the shepherds' response to this news of great joy at the birth of Jesus?

"Away in a Manger"
Author: 1st 2 stanzas, unknown;
stanza 3, John Thomas McFarland, 1892

Away in a manger, no crib for a bed,
The little Lord Jesus laid down His sweet head.
The stars in the sky looked down where He lay,
The little Lord Jesus, asleep on the hay.

The cattle are lowing, the Baby awakes,
But little Lord Jesus, no crying He makes;
I love Thee, Lord Jesus, look down from the sky
And stay by my cradle til morning is nigh.

Be near me, Lord Jesus, I ask Thee to stay
Close by me forever, and love me, I pray;
Bless all the dear children in Thy tender care,
And fit us for Heaven to live with Thee there.

Prayer

The joy You have brought us, Lord, is exceedingly great. We believe the message of the angel about the coming of Christ into the world and we look forward to celebrating this event. Thank You for bringing us such joy. In Jesus' name, Amen.

December 22   **Surprise! When God Became Man**

In the beginning was the Word, and the Word was with God, and the Word was God. He was in the beginning with God. All things were made through him, and without him was not any thing made that was made.... And the Word became flesh and dwelt among us, and we have seen his glory, glory as of the only Son from the Father, full of grace and truth. (John 1:1-3, 14)

We have certain expectations in life. We expect the sun to rise every day. We anticipate plenty of oxygen in the air to keep us alive. We look for new leaders in society every few years, as older leaders retire or get replaced. We count on our vehicle's engine to start when we turn the key or push the button for ignition. We get ready for cramped quarters on airplane flights (or it is only uncomfortable for us with long legs and broad shoulders). The list is endless. Each generation has similar expectations. No one, however, expected God to become human. And yet, that's just what He did in the Person of Jesus Christ.

It's no surprise God is eternal, for He existed before the creation of space and time. When we look to the beginning of time, God was already there: "In the beginning God..." (Genesis 1:1). As challenging as it is for us to think about eternity past, we can grasp something of the eternal nature of God—He had to exist to become the Creator of the universe. The Word is this Creator God. The Apostle John is clear about the full deity of the Word.

Then, more than 2,000 years ago, this Creator literally stepped into the world He created and became a human—the Word became flesh. He remained fully God and added full humanity.

While He could have just made a U-turn back to heaven, He didn't. He "dwelt among us." This phrase conveys the notion of the Word "making a tabernacle" or "pitching His tent" in our world, playing off the era when the glory of God filled the tabernacle among Israel. Whenever the cloud of the glory of Yahweh moved out, Israel would pack up the tent and follow. Whenever God's glory remained, God's people stayed next to the tent put in place. Moses wrote, "For the cloud of the LORD was on the tabernacle by day, and fire was in it by night, in the sight of all the house of Israel throughout all their journeys" (Exodus 40:38).

So the Apostle John tells us the Word which became flesh and pitched His tent in our world is the manifestation of God's glory which led Israel in the wilderness. John and others witnessed this glory of the One and Only Son of the Father. Though older translations use "Only Begotten Son," too many people misunderstand the concept, thinking it refers to a metaphysical relationship. This phrase refers to Christ as the Only Unique Son, for the same phrase occurs with reference to Abraham's son Isaac (Hebrews 11:17) and Isaac certainly was not Abraham's only begotten son. He was, however, Abraham's only unique son, given to him by God's promise.

This Word-made-flesh, or God-Man, is full of grace and truth. Both concepts are important to the Christian faith, for grace is God's favor bestowed on undeserving people. Truth comes from God and is central to John's teaching (the words for *true*, *truthful* and *truth* occur 68 times in John's writings). It relates to God's faithfulness and reliability and connects to the cross of Christ. Just before Jesus' crucifixion, Pilate asked Jesus, "What is truth?" (John 18:38). Though Jesus did not give him an answer in words, He gave him an answer with His works by dying and rising as demonstration of His truthful identity as God's Messiah.

To repeat my claim above, *no one* expected God to become man. But the Word, the Son of God, did just that. But come to think of it, God is the God of the unexpected. No one expected a child to be born of a virgin. No one expected a Man from Nazareth to make claims of being the Messiah. No one expected the crucified Man from Nazareth to rise from the dead. But God did all those things in Jesus. I, for one, am glad God surprised the world and did the unexpected.

God heard His people and their many tear-filled cries
And the Word became flesh, much to our own surprise,
To live among people, much like a tent or booth,
He's God's Only Unique Son, full of grace and truth.

Application Idea

Have you ever been surprised? How did it make you feel? Think of a way to surprise someone else close to you—a spouse, your children, a good friend (maybe an unexpected gift). Afterwards, tell them of God's surprise for the world when He became the God-Man Jesus Christ.

"Come, Thou Almighty King"
Author: Felice de Giardini, c. 1756

Come, Thou almighty King,
Help us Thy name to sing, help us to praise!
Father all glorious, o'er all victorious,
Come and reign over us, Ancient of Days!

Come, Thou incarnate Word,
Gird on Thy mighty sword, our prayer attend!
Come, and Thy people bless, and give Thy Word success,
Spirit of holiness, on us descend!

Come, holy Comforter,
Thy sacred witness bear in this glad hour.
Thou who almighty art, now rule in every heart,
And ne'er from us depart, Spirit of power!

To Thee, great One in Three,
Eternal praises be, hence, evermore.
Thy sovereign majesty may we in glory see,
And to eternity love and adore!

Prayer

God, thank You for surprising us in marvelous ways. You are in control of history and that gives us comfort. Jesus, thank You for walking in our shoes and being our sacrifice for sin. We pray in Your name, Amen.

December 23   The Good, the Bad and the Ugly in Family

The book of the genealogy of Jesus Christ, the son of David, the son of Abraham. Abraham was the father of Isaac.... and Jacob the father of Joseph the husband of Mary, of whom Jesus was born, who is called Christ. (Matthew 1:1-2, 16)

Do you ever find yourself looking around at your family members at Thanksgiving or Christmas and wonder how *you* could be related to *them*? I'm not talking about your *in-laws* but your own *blood relatives*! Let's face it: no family is perfect and every family has its share of good people, bad people and ugly people. As a matter of fact, take a close look at yourself. Would you describe yourself as good? How about bad? If neither of those fits you, then guess what? You're *ugly*!

But don't worry. The Lord has a way of working wonders in the lives of such people. Look at the genealogy of Jesus in Matthew 1. You certainly find some rather prominent, good members of Jesus' family, including Abraham, Isaac, Jacob, Judah, Boaz, Ruth, David, Solomon, Josiah and Zerubbabel.

But you also discover something else: bad, dark, ugly histories of many of Jesus' ancestors. While we don't know much about many of Jesus' forefathers, of those we know, almost all of them are marked by notable moral failures. Even the "good" guys have a "bad" and "ugly" appearance. For example, Abraham lied about his wife, as did Isaac; Jacob was a deceiver; Judah was a fornicator with Tamar; Rahab was a Canaanite prostitute; David was an adulterer with Bathsheba. Solomon put the *poly* in *polygamist* (many/multiple wives)! I wonder how he kept up with the birthdays and anniversaries of 1,000 wives, princesses and concubines! And how did he manage all of those mothers-in-law? Solomon's son, Rehoboam, divided the kingdom. Manasseh was the most evil king Israel ever had.

Even Jechoniah (Jehoiachin) was cursed by God so that he would be as though "childless, a man who shall not succeed in his days, for none of his offspring shall succeed in sitting on the throne of David and ruling again in Judah" (Jeremiah 22:30). The house of David had become so evil God cut them off from the throne, which would be vacant for 600 years before Christ. Although God took away any hope man had put in himself, God remained faithful to His promise to send a Davidic descendant to reign in righteousness. Jesus is a demonstration of God's mercy toward His people for He came to "save his people from their sins" (Matthew 1:21).

Have you ever researched your family tree? I find a good deal of interest in my family, but my Dad's side is virtually impossible to trace beyond a few generations because of all the variant spellings of my last name. I can map out a branch through my Mom's side to at least the middle 18th century. When we track our family's history, we inevitably run across people who were adulterers, drunkards, murderers, prisoners and more. Though we might want to run from our past, we cannot escape it, whether it is our family or the face in the mirror. Some of us dread holiday gatherings because we see people in our family who bring up bad memories— an abusive father, a drug-addict uncle, an adulterous aunt.

That's why Jesus Christ is so significant and Matthew is ingenious in recording Jesus' genealogy. Our families and our lives are not too different from Jesus' family and just as He came to give hope to them and deliver His family from their sinful pasts, so He can give hope and do the same for you. So whether you are the good, the bad or the ugly in your family, Jesus is your hope!

> Why don't you take a look at your own family,
> And you will see the good, bad and even ugly?
> Then cling to the Lord Jesus, who saves you from sin
> And provides you a new life to begin again.

Application Idea

What do you know about your ancestors (you may not want to go into too many negative details for your children)? Were they good? Which ones were bad? Were any just plain ugly? Now what about your life—are there some bad and ugly things mixed in it? Have you turned from your sinful past and trusted in Jesus to save you from your sins?

"Good Christian Men, Rejoice"
Origin: 14th Century Latin;
Translator: John Mason Neale, c. 1853

Good Christian men, rejoice
With heart and soul and voice!
Give ye heed to what we say:
Jesus Christ is born today!
Man and beast before Him bow,
And He is in the manger now:
Christ was born today,
Christ was born today!

Good Christian men, rejoice
With heart and soul and voice!
Now ye hear of endless bliss:
Jesus Christ was born for this!
He has opened heaven's door,
And man is blest forevermore.
Christ was born for this,
Christ was born for this!

Good Christian men, rejoice
With heart and soul and voice!
Now ye need not fear the grave:
Jesus Christ was born to save!
Calls you one and calls you all
To gain His everlasting hall.
Christ was born to save,
Christ was born to save!

Prayer

Dear Jesus, thank You for coming into the world to save Your
people from their sins, including me and my family. Give us the
strength to live in a manner worthy of being called Your people.
We ask these things in Your name, Amen.

CELEBRATING THE PROMISE

JOEL BREIDENBAUGH

December 24   Gifts Fit for a King

When [the wise men] saw the star, they rejoiced exceedingly with great joy. And going into the house they saw the child with Mary his mother, and they fell down and worshiped him. Then, opening their treasures, they offered him gifts, gold and frankincense and myrrh. (Matthew 2:10-11)

How many times have you wanted to shop for others and you knew you couldn't afford what you wanted to give them? Or have you ever exchanged Christmas gifts with family or friends and realized you spent far less on their gift than what they spent on you? Depending on the contrast between the gifts, you may have feelings of embarrassment, guilt, humiliation, shame, uneasiness and the like.

Now what if you tried to present a gift to the President of the United States? Or what if you tried to offer a present to a billionaire? He could buy whatever he wants, why should you give him anything? The greater reason for giving gifts to those you love is not so much *what* you give as *that* you give. Hear me out: I'm not saying *what* you give isn't important, but it isn't as important as *that* you give something.

A long, long time ago, in a country far away, some wise men traveled a considerable distance to meet Jesus, the King of the Jews. They had followed His star until they ended up in Bethlehem, where they entered a house and met Jesus. These wise men do what you expect them to do before a king, they lay prostrate before Him. And they worship Him.

Huh? Wait a minute. Do you mean to tell me a group of Gentiles worship the King of the Jews? Surely something is wrong here. Matthew is a Jew writing primarily to Jews and they take worship seriously. Not only did they have the first two commandments against worshipping anyone/thing but Yahweh, but they also were severely judged whenever they worshipped other gods. From a Jewish perspective, you'd expect Matthew to add "but God struck the wise men with a plague and they were eaten by worms, because they wrongly worshipped Jesus." But Matthew has already labeled Jesus Immanuel, God with us (1:23). So the wise men's worship of Jesus is right.

And one way they express their worship is in giving gifts—gold, frankincense and myrrh.

> Gold, a precious metal valued higher than all others;
> Frankincense, a resinous gum from trees in Arabia, was used medicinally;
> Myrrh, also a resinous gum used medicinally (when mixed with wine, as a narcotic, Mark 15:23; for prolonging a body's decay in burial, John 19:39).

Each of these gifts were valuable commodities in the first century (see Revelation 18:11-13). They were among gifts the "best money could buy." Because of his wealth, a king doesn't typically need such gifts, but these gifts were acceptable to the Lord, because they were the best these wise men could offer.

We are not certain all Matthew intended to communicate with these gifts. Many preachers have claimed the gold represented royalty, frankincense expressed deity and myrrh looked to Jesus' suffering and death, but Matthew doesn't underscore these things. God may have been revealing these truths through the rest of the New Testament, but we don't discover them in Matthew.

We don't know what happened with these gifts. If they were given to our child at birth, we might sale them and start a college fund or we may try to put them in a special place. Such actions were not taken in the ancient Near East. Joseph and Mary probably sold the gifts as a way to finance their trip to Egypt (see 2:13-15).

Regardless of what was done with the gifts, the wise men had taught Jesus' parents and future readers of this account a very important lesson about Jesus: in Him "are hidden all the treasures of wisdom and knowledge" (Colossians 2:3). Since Jesus is God's greatest gift to us, it is only right for our greatest gifts to be the best gifts for Jesus, for they are gifts fit for a King!

> Gift-giving is 'specially great this time each year,
> For it reminds us God's greatest Gift has come near.
> He gave us His very best, His own life for us,
> It's only right to worship Him as King Jesus!

Application Idea

Search online for the song "Little Drummer Boy" and listen to one of the versions. Did the boy have much to offer Jesus? How is his gift of playing his drum important for us? What do you have or what can you do to offer something to Jesus in worship as your king?

"We Three Kings of Orient Are"
Author: John Henry Hopkins, Jr., 1857

We three kings of Orient are:
Bearing gifts we traverse afar,
Field and fountain, moor and mountain,
Following yonder star.

Refrain
O star of wonder, star of light,
Star with royal beauty bright,
Westward leading, still proceeding,
Guide us to thy perfect light.

Born a King on Bethlehem's plain
Gold I bring to crown Him again,
King forever, ceasing never,
Over us all to reign.

Frankincense to offer have I;
Incense owns a Deity nigh;
Prayer and praising, voices raising,
Worshipping God on high.

Myrrh is mine, its bitter perfume
Breathes a life of gathering gloom;
Sorrowing, sighing, bleeding, dying,
Sealed in the stone cold tomb.

Glorious now behold Him arise;
King and God and sacrifice;
Alleluia, Alleluia,
Sounds through the earth and skies.

Prayer
Jesus, You are worthy of the very best gifts we can give You. May we always be ready to give You our lives in service, for we serve the King. We pray these things in Your name, Amen.

December 25   Peace on Earth!

And suddenly there was with the angel a multitude of the heavenly host praising God and saying, "Glory to God in the highest, and on earth peace among those with whom he is pleased! (Luke 2:13-14)

'Tis the season to be honest; okay, I admit it: one of my favorite Christmas songs is by the Royal Guardsmen entitled "Snoopy's Christmas." I guess I like the tune and spirit of it all—Americans and Germans celebrating Christmas together in the midst of a world war. My kids and I also get a kick out of the clips from "A Charlie Brown Christmas" set to the song on YouTube. In case you are unfamiliar with the song, its chorus goes, "Christmas bells, those Christmas bells, Ringing through the land, Bringing peace to all the world, and goodwill to man."

Like it or not, the song is a bit misleading. Christmas bells do not bring "peace to *all* the world" nor "goodwill to man." Christmas itself doesn't even do that, but the meaning behind it— the coming of Christ into this world to save sinners—brings peace. But is that peace automatic? And what's this part about *goodwill?*

You probably realize that this song comes from the heavenly choir from Luke's Gospel: "Glory to God in the highest, and on earth peace, good will toward men" (2:14). That's the King James Version's rendering, but the latter portion of the verse can be misunderstood. The former part—"Glory to God in the highest"—is a declaration of praise and worship to the Most High God. Other translations have sought to clarify the latter part: "on earth peace toward men of goodwill" or "peace among those with whom He is pleased" or even "peace on earth to people He favors."

"Peace" seems obvious enough. It is the harmony or well-being between two or more parties (who may have been at odds with each other at an earlier time). The peace in Scripture often refers to the peace believers have with God through His reconciling work. Being at peace with God means you have a right standing with Him. Paul says it well: "We implore you on behalf of Christ, be reconciled to God. For our sake he [God] made him [Christ] to be sin who knew no sin, so that in him [Christ] we might become the righteousness of God" (2 Corinthians 5:20-21). This passage contains one of the greatest theological truths ever:

God transferred our sin onto Christ at His death. Furthermore, Christ's righteousness is transferred onto us. That righteousness, which gives us a right standing with God, only comes if we are "in Christ," meaning we must trust in Him. So, even though we were once separated from and enemies of God, He has brought us near through the work of Christ and we now have peace with Him.

Such peace makes perfect sense with "goodwill toward men." The idea of goodwill highlights God's favor, His grace. Those who have His grace are those who have received the gift of Jesus Christ by faith. Indeed, recipients of God's grace are at peace with Him and those at peace with God have His favor rest on them—they are two sides of the same coin.

So the way you, or anyone on earth, can have real peace is by trusting in Christ as the only sufficient sacrifice for your sins, by receiving God's gift of grace. In light of this special news, we may appreciate Christmas bells this time of year and really have a Merry Christmas!

> So let the beautiful Christmas bells loudly ring!
> And let host of angelic choirs of heaven sing!
> We can now have peace in our lives upon this earth,
> As long as we treasure Christ as our greatest worth!

Application Idea
If you keep a diary, write down what Christmas means to you. If you don't keep one, consider a holiday journal by jotting down some thoughts on important days—Christmas, Thanksgiving, Easter, New Year's and other special days in your life. You may want to tape pictures of the day inside the journal as an extra reminder of the good times God has given you.

"I Heard the Bells on Christmas Day"
Author: Henry W. Longfellow, 1863

> I heard the bells on Christmas day
> Their old familiar carols play,
> And wild and sweet the words repeat
> Of peace on earth, good will to men.

And thought how, as the day had come,
The belfries of all Christendom
Had rolled along th'unbroken song
Of peace on earth, good will to men.

And in despair I bowed my head
"There is no peace on earth," I said,
"For hate is strong and mocks the song
Of peace on earth, good will to men."

Then pealed the bells more loud and deep:
"God is not dead, nor doth He sleep;
The wrong shall fail, the right prevail
With peace on earth, good will to men."

Till, ringing, singing on its way,
The world revolved from night to day,
A voice, a chime, a chant sublime
Of peace on earth, good will to men.

Prayer

God, thank You for Your grace and peace found in a right relationship with You by faith in Your Son Jesus. You give me much to sing about in praise to You. In Jesus' name, Amen.

December 26   **News Worth Sharing**

... the shepherds said to one another, "Let us go over to Bethlehem and see this thing that has happened, which the Lord has made known to us." And they went with haste and found Mary and Joseph, and the baby lying in a manger. And when they saw it, they made known the saying that had been told them concerning this child." (Luke 2:15-17)

Shepherds. Not a very impressive bunch. Shepherds don't conjure up thoughts of grandeur. Several types of figures throughout history spark immediate thoughts of greatness.

      Kings: authority.

      Scholars: intelligence.

      Veterans: honor.

      Athletes: strength.

      Fathers: respect.

      Mothers: love.

      Entertainers: fame.

      Shepherds: huh?

Shepherds don't seem to fit the storyline. Throughout these readings, you've read about David and a future king, wise men and even angels. That's the stuff movies are made of. But shepherds? While we know that shepherds had to protect, watch over, provide and care for their flocks, the occupation of shepherd does not saturate the dreams of little boys and girls.

But it gets worse. Shepherds in ancient Israel were often associated with lawbreakers and thieves. Because their occupation demanded round-the-clock care, shepherds usually could not keep all of the ceremonial laws. Add to that the fact that shepherds often had a hard time distinguishing between "mine" and "thine," and you begin to see the kinds of accusations leveled at shepherds, even by their own kind. Because of these types of blemishes, shepherds were among the lowest class of society. Kind of sets things in a humble surrounding, don't you think?

Yet shepherds are the first to receive the good news from an angel about a special baby's birth in the city of David, "a Savior, who is Christ the Lord" (Luke 2:11). They immediately travel to the city of David, Bethlehem, to see what the Lord had made known to them. Had we been present, you and I would be pushing each other over to get to town as fast as we could. News about the

Messianic Deliverer gets any Jewish person's attention.

When the shepherds arrived, they became eyewitnesses of the promise of the Lord. The greatest of David's sons was right before their very eyes. Such reality was no small matter. Though David's offspring had sat on the throne for hundreds of years after King David, it had been hundreds of years since the Jewish kingdom had been overthrown. Though many of David's family members had come and gone, the Israelites were still waiting for God to restore the kingdom by putting Christ, the ultimate Son of David, on the throne throughout all time.

So what do we have? A prophecy was made and a tiny village selected. A clear angelic message was given to low-class shepherds. What does this mean? The promises of God can affect everyone from kings to shepherds, the top of the upper-class to the bottom of the lower-class. That includes you and me. God must have a special plan to bring us all together. And this news is too great not to share with others.

> News like this, so great, I certainly cannot keep
> It to myself, nor should I be able to sleep
> Another moment longer until I do find
> This Savior—Christ the Lord—may He e'er fill my mind!

Application Idea
Bake some cookies or take a box of chocolates to a shut-in (who may not see many family members or friends at Christmas). Help them take down their Christmas decorations. Or volunteer a few hours at a local soup kitchen in feeding the homeless. Whatever you do, help spread the joy Christ has given you to others in need.

"Go, Tell It on the Mountain"
Author: John W. Work, Jr., c. 1865

Chorus:
Go, tell it on the mountain,
Over the hills and ev'rywhere;
Go, tell it on the mountain
That Jesus Christ is born!

While shepherds kept their watching
O'er silent flocks by night,
Behold throughout the heavens
There shone a holy light.

The shepherds feared and trembled
When lo! above the earth
Rang out the angel chorus
That hailed our Savior's birth.

Down in a lowly manger
The humble Christ was born,
And God sent us salvation
That blessed Christmas morn.

Prayer

Lord, You have blessed us with the message of the good news of Jesus and You have commanded us to share this message with others. Help us as we seek to be faithful to You. In Jesus' name we ask these things, Amen.

December 27   **Waiting on the Lord**

[Simeon] was righteous and devout, waiting for the consolation of Israel, and the Holy Spirit was upon him. And it had been revealed to him by the Holy Spirit that he would not see death before he had seen the Lord's Christ. And he came in the Spirit into the temple, and when the parents brought in the child Jesus, to do for him according to the custom of the Law, he took him up in his arms and blessed God and said, "Lord, now you are letting your servant depart in peace, according to your word…" (Luke 2:25b-29)

Waiting. From the time we are kids until well into adulthood, we have a problem with waiting. Your children may have trouble waiting on the rest of the family to be seated before they start eating. Husbands will accumulate days and weeks (maybe even months and years!) while waiting on their wives to shop. Wives will wait on their husbands to finish watching their ball game. Church-goers wait on the preacher to finish his sermon. Metropolitans wait on traffic to get to and from work. The list could go on. Much of our lives are spent waiting. And most of us don't like it, because we've developed a fast-food mentality to all of life—I want it… *now!*

There are risks to waiting on some things. Waiting in traffic may cause you to miss a meeting or an important appointment. Waiting on a husband and father to show up late from work may mean missing a hot meal. Waiting on a no-show bride at a wedding could be the end of a relationship. I waited nearly two hours to get autographs of some of my favorite baseball players at a spring training game. I didn't get a single one. But I did get some minor league players' autographs—not what I wanted, but it thrilled my boys to get any player's autograph, so it was worth the wait.

I can't help but wonder if the Lord makes us wait on routine things in life to teach us about waiting on Him. Take Simeon, for example. There's a whole lot we don't know about him—his family, his vocation, his age. Luke apportions a mere 1% of his Gospel (11 verses out of 1,151) to this man. He gets a brief introduction (2:25-28), offers a prayer of praise to God (2:29-32) and provides a few prophetic words to Mary concerning Jesus (2:33-35). That's it. But there's more here than meets the eye.

The Jewish people as a whole have learned to wait on the Lord. Yahweh promised Abram a son when he was 75 years old and *25 years later*, Isaac was born to him. Jacob worked *fourteen years* to secure Rachel as his wife. The Israelites were in bondage in Egypt for *several centuries* before Yahweh redeemed them through Moses. *For hundreds and thousands of years*, the Jews waited for God to send His Messiah (first promised to Eve and reiterated many times throughout the centuries). Since Malachi had prophesied, God was silent *for over 400 years*. He didn't say a word. The people waited to hear from Him.

Therefore, when Simeon waited "for the consolation of Israel," he was waiting on the Lord to bring comfort, just like so many of his ancestors had done. Then the Spirit of God revealed to Simeon that their waiting was coming to an end and he would get to be an eyewitness of the Messiah before he died! Can you imagine his excitement? All the waiting was almost over. The Messiah would come in Simeon's lifetime!

It shouldn't surprise us to find Simeon in Jerusalem at the temple. The Spirit of God led this child of God to the house of God to witness the Son of God! Appropriately, upon seeing and holding Jesus in his arms, Simeon praises God for fulfilling His promise. As a slave who has fulfilled his task to his Master, Simeon then asks to be released from his earthly post of service, ready to depart in peace and be with God. Simeon had been waiting on God to send the Messiah to bring comfort and peace to Israel. With that mission completed, Simeon was prepared to die in peace, confident he had carried out his assignment from God.

Simeon's waiting had paid off. Though he risked missing out on other things in life by going to the temple that day, nothing was more important for him to do. So it is with us. We have to wait on the Lord and His timing. Like Simeon, let's be faithful in devotion to our Lord. Whatever else may come our way, looking to and learning from Christ will be worth the wait.

> Many of us surely don't prefer a long wait,
> But when it's all over, it's time to celebrate!
> God's timing is perfect in ev'ry single way
> So let's be found waiting on Him until that Day.

Application Idea

What are some things you have to wait on regularly? How does it make you feel? How do your (grand)kids adjust to waiting for Christmas each year? What are some benefits to waiting?

"The Birthday of a King"
Author: William Harold Neidlinger, 1890

In the little village of Bethlehem,
There lay a Child one day,
And the sky was bright with a holy light
O'er the place where Jesus lay.

Refrain:
Alleluia! O how the angels sang.
Alleluia! How it rang!
And the sky was bright with a holy light
'Twas the birthday of a King.

'Twas a humble birthplace, but O how much
God gave to us that day,
From the manger bed what a path has led,
What a perfect, holy way.

Prayer

Help us, O Lord, to wait on You. You know what's best for us and You are faithful to keep Your word. Though we grow weary in the wait sometimes, we really want to trust You. Help us in this wait, we ask in Jesus' name, Amen.

December 28   A Tale of Two Kings

Now after Jesus was born in Bethlehem of Judea in the days of Herod the king, behold, wise men from the east came to Jerusalem, saying, "Where is he who has been born king of the Jews? For we saw his star when it rose and have come to worship Him." (Matthew 2:1-2)

"It was the best of times, it was the worst of times, it was the age of wisdom, it was the age of foolishness, it was the epoch of belief, it was the epoch of incredulity, it was the season of Light, it was the season of Darkness, it was the spring of hope, it was the winter of despair..." These opening words to Charles Dickens 1889 classic *The Tale of Two Cities* refer to life in England and France in 1775. Indeed, many changes lay on the horizon. The American Revolution would inspire the French in just a few years. The nations, as they were known then, would never be the same.

In an even greater contrast, the coming of Jesus Christ into the world as the King of the Jews in the days of King Herod certainly underscored two vastly different kings. The latter went down in the pages of history as King Herod the Great. The former still receives attention today, not simply as the King of the Jews, but also as the Savior of the world and the Lord of all.

Dickens' words could easily apply to "The Tale of Two Kings." The *best of times* were fast-approaching for the Jewish people, as their Messiah was stepping into the world. The *worst of times* were coming to an end, when they no longer had to wait for God to fulfill His promise—Roman rule would not have the final word. It was the *age of wisdom* as Jesus became "wisdom from God" for His followers (1 Corinthians 1:30). It was the *age of foolishness* as the religious leaders of first-century Palestine entrapped people with burdensome laws. It was the *epoch of belief* for believers chosen by God "to be saved, through sanctification by the Spirit and belief in the truth" (2 Thessalonians 2:13). It was the *epoch of incredulity* as many disbelieved the gospel of God's grace in Christ (cf. Acts 28:24). It was the *season of Light* for all who saw Jesus as "the light of the world" (John 8:12), but it was the *season of Darkness* for any who were not in fellowship with God (cf. 1 John 1:6). It was the *spring of hope* because of Jesus' resurrection from the dead (1 Peter 1:3), yet it was the *winter of despair* for everyone who sought meaning in life outside of Christ.

The reason the era of first-century Palestine was marked by foolishness, despair and more had much to do with King Herod. Although known for rebuilding the temple in Jerusalem, Herod levied high taxes on his subjects, burdening them with his pet projects in Caesarea Maritima and his fortresses and palaces in Jerusalem, Jericho, Herodium and Masada. Herod was also ruthless in his dealings with others. Not only did he order little boys to be killed in Bethlehem (he assumed he accomplished his mission of murdering the King of the Jews), but he also killed his father-in-law, several of his ten wives, and three sons. When the end of his life was approaching, Herod issued orders to execute multiple family members upon his death so that all the people would really mourn (those orders were not performed). Herod may have been "the Great," but he was great in evil. Once in a Christmas pageant, a little boy had trouble annunciating his words and referred to him as "King Horrid." The boy was more accurate than he realized.

That same time period carried great hope, too, with the entrance of Jesus. Though born to a humble family who made their living as carpenters, Jesus wasn't known for building vast palaces and fortresses. The majority of His work as a young adult may have been constructing wooden scaffolding for stonemasons. Far from skilled professionals today, carpenters in Jesus' day were below peasant farmers. Take into consideration the fact there were but two classes in society then—the wealthy and the peasants—and you can see Jesus in the lower half of the poor. He didn't even have a home (cf. Matthew 8:20). But none of those things prevented Jesus from fulfilling His God-given mission to live a sinless life, die a sacrificial death for sinners, and rise from the dead to prove He is the Son of God and King of the world. Unlike Herod, Jesus is truly a great King, a King worth following!

> Even though he was known as King Herod the Great
> His death caused him to be simply Herod the Late.
> Yet now Jesus the Poor has become so much more
> For He died, rose again and reigns forevermore!

Application Idea
Take an evening ride with your family and find some Christmas lights and decorations in a neighborhood. In a sense, how do the decorations portray two different worlds or two different

kingdoms? How would you contrast this world and heaven?

"O Worship the King"
Author: Robert Grant, 1833

O worship the King, all glorious above,
O gratefully sing His power and His love;
Our Shield and Defender, the Ancient of Days,
Pavilioned in splendor, and girded with praise.

O tell of His might, O sing of His grace,
Whose robe is the light, whose canopy space,
His chariots of wrath the deep thunderclouds form,
And dark is His path on the wings of the storm.

The earth with its store of wonders untold,
Almighty, Thy power hath founded of old;
Established it fast by a changeless decree,
And round it hath cast, like a mantle, the sea.

Thy bountiful care, what tongue can recite?
It breathes in the air, it shines in the light;
It streams from the hills, it descends to the plain,
And sweetly distills in the dew and the rain.

Frail children of dust, and feeble as frail,
In Thee do we trust, nor find Thee to fail;
Thy mercies how tender, how firm to the end,
Our Maker, Defender, Redeemer, and Friend.

O measureless might! Ineffable love!
While angels delight to worship Thee above,
The humbler creation, though feeble their lays,
With true adoration shall all sing Thy praise.

Prayer

Father in heaven, though we are so often torn by this world, enable us to live in view of the kingdom Christ is building, for we pray this in His name, Amen.

December 29   Close to Christmas, But Far from Christ

... Wise men from the east came to Jerusalem.... Then Herod summoned the wise men secretly and ascertained from them what time the star had appeared. And he sent them to Bethlehem, saying, "Go and search diligently for the child, and when you have found him, bring me word, that I too may come and worship him." (Matthew 2:1, 7-8)

Have you ever trusted a GPS to get you where you needed to go, only to discover the destination was incorrect? One reason I prefer looking at an old-fashioned road map is because I'm accustomed to it and I've had one-too-many failed experiences with a GPS. On at least one occasion, I never found what I was looking for. I wonder how close I was.

The church I have the privilege of serving has annual Christmas Eve services. We have huge crowds attend, some out of devotion to our Lord, some out of family obligation or expectation. Every year I notice something about the people. They have all turned out to celebrate the Christmas season. They are literally hours from Christmas day. But for several individuals, they don't really get it. They are close to Christmas and its true meaning, but they are far from Christ, because they don't really know Him.

A similar near-far proximity existed around Jesus. While many would "rub shoulders" with Him during His ministry, they were a "million miles away" from Him, because they didn't recognize Him as the Messiah. For these people, their blindness seems inexcusable—they heard His teaching and saw His miracles. How could they miss the obvious? They were so close and yet so far away.

Of course, the short-sightedness of people concerning Christ began right after his birth. Wise men came to Jerusalem seeking the One "born King of the Jews" (Messiah) for they had followed His star. When King Herod heard this news, he gathered the resident theologians to ask where the Messiah would be born. They pointed Herod to Bethlehem, referencing Micah's prophecy eight centuries earlier (see December 6 above). Herod responds by trying to figure the timing of the Messiah's birth—when did the star appear?

What happens next is somewhat stunning: Herod sent the wise men off and commanded them to return to him once they found the child. What's so stunning about that? Bethlehem is only

6 miles from Jerusalem. Though the land is mountainous, you can travel between Jerusalem and Bethlehem by foot in a single day. Now I know Herod was king, and as king, he had plenty to keep him occupied. He may not have had time to travel himself. But then again, since he was king, he could have postponed his activities and made the journey to Bethlehem himself. Or he could have sent some Roman soldiers along with the wise men, giving them secret orders to carry out his murderous intentions. Or some of the theologians could have gone and returned to Herod, anticipating financial gain.

But no, neither Herod nor his soldiers nor the religious leaders would make this trek. Not at this time. They would depend on the wise men to do the hard work of tracking down the child, counting on them to return with the whereabouts of the Messiah's location. Scholars don't know the exact origin of the wise men, but they were probably from Persia, though they could have come from India or China. The wise men could have traveled as little as 800 miles to get to Jerusalem, and they may have covered over 2,000 miles! Another six miles for them was nothing, a skip in the park. They traversed the land, found the child and worshipped Jesus as the Christ.

The difference between Herod (and the religious leaders) and the wise men paints a portrait seen many places today. With each passing year, Christmas comes and goes. People darken the doors of churches and hear how Christ came to change the world, a message not far away, but near (cf. Romans 10:8). But unless they come to Christ in faith, like the wise men, they may be close to Christmas, but they are far from Christ.

> The Christmas event comes around this time each year
> And people listen to carols and gather near
> To hear of Jesus, then they travel home by car
> Living for themselves. Close to Christ? No, they are far.

Application Idea
Use your GPS to go somewhere you've never been (you may only want to go a few miles). Was it trustworthy? Have you ever come close to something, only to miss it? Do you regret it? How did Herod and his people regret traveling to see the Messiah?

"Jesus, Keep Me Near the Cross"
Author: Fanny Crosby, 1869

Jesus, keep me near the cross,
There a precious fountain
Free to all, a healing stream
Flows from Calvary's mountain.

Refrain
In the cross, in the cross,
Be my glory ever;
Till my raptured soul shall find
Rest beyond the river.

Near the cross, a trembling soul,
Love and mercy found me;
There the bright and morning star
Sheds its beams around me.

Near the cross! O Lamb of God,
Bring its scenes before me;
Help me walk from day to day,
With its shadows o'er me.

Near the cross I'll watch and wait
Hoping, trusting ever,
Till I reach the golden strand,
Just beyond the river.

Prayer

O Jesus, please keep me near You and the cross upon which You died. Don't let me miss the real meaning of this annual holiday. Though I was once far off, You drew me near. Thank You. I pray in Your name, Amen.

December 30   **The Sorrow of the Season**

Then Herod, when he saw that he had been tricked by the wise men, became furious, and he sent and killed all the male children in Bethlehem and in all that region who were two years old and under, according to the time that he had ascertained from the wise men. Then was fulfilled what was spoken by the prophet Jeremiah: "A voice was heard in Ramah, weeping and loud lamentation, Rachel weeping for her children; she refused to be comforted, because they are no more." (Matthew 2:16-18)

Do you ever stop to think about people who experience sorrow each Christmas? Maybe you are one of those people, because you lost a loved one during the Christmas season, or one well before his/her time, and every family gathering now has a void. You are not alone.

The coming of Christ into the world (what you might call the first Christmas, though it would be some time before the world recognized it) has brought tremendous joy to great multitudes, beginning with Mary and Joseph. But everyone did not rejoice when Christ came into the world. Several families were preoccupied with sorrow over the loss of their own little ones.

You know the story: the wise men, following a star, come to Jerusalem to inquire about the newly born King of the Jews. King Herod the Great summons his scribes, who inform the wise men about Bethlehem as the birthplace of the coming Messiah. Herod instructs the wise men to find the child and return with a report so he, too, could worship him. The wise men go to Bethlehem, find the Child Jesus, worship him and leave, being warned in a dream not to return to Herod. After some time had passed, Herod realizes the wise men aren't returning and gets raging mad, so mad he orders all little boys in the region of Bethlehem, newborn through two years of age, to be slaughtered. We know the order was carried out, because Matthew notes the fulfillment of prophecy and sees Rachel as a metaphor for weeping mothers (Jeremiah 31:15). Scholars tell us there were probably about one dozen boys in this age range in the region of Bethlehem at that time. That's twelve hurting families in a small town around the time Christ entered the world.

I wonder how the Roman soldiers performed this atrocity. Did they storm into homes and ask for small boys? Did they imply they wanted to honor the son, only to kill him? Did they trick the families into giving up their sons, unsure of what was to occur? The Bible doesn't tell us *how* they were killed, only *that* they were killed. The toddler may have been playing with a toy one minute, only to come face to face with a sword the next minute. Surely it was the slaughter of the innocents.

But there is more to this story, and it includes hope and cause for celebration. Matthew's reference to Jeremiah pointed to Ramah, a town where the Jewish captives were deported to Babylon (Jeremiah 40:1). Rachel was the mother of Joseph (father of Ephraim [northern kingdom]) and Benjamin (southern kingdom). She represents all Israel crying over her children taken as prisoners to a foreign land. That was surely a reason to mourn.

Yet here's where there's cause for hope. The context of Jeremiah's prophecy of Rachel's sorrow includes what "Thus says the LORD: 'Keep your voice from weeping, and your eyes from tears, for there is a reward for your work, declares the LORD, and they shall come back from the land of the enemy. There is hope for your future, declares the LORD, and your children shall come back to their own country'" (31:16-17).

Okay, but this refers to children taken in captivity. The little boys in Jesus' day were killed and couldn't return. But they could go on to heaven. Jesus said about children, "See that you do not despise one of these little ones. For I tell you that in heaven their angels always see the face of my Father who is in heaven" (Matthew 18:10). Jesus then adds a statement about the shepherd's joy at finding his lost sheep, an analogy about preserving little children. The conclusion is straightforward: "So it is not the will of my Father who is in heaven that one of these little ones should perish" (18:14). The word "perish" means to be cut off for all eternity (i.e. sent to hell). Jesus says that it isn't God's will for a little one to go to hell.[1]

Even King David experienced losing a child and had hope in seeing him again (cf. 2 Samuel 12:15-23). He knew sorrow could turn into celebration, for he wrote, "Weeping may tarry for the night, but joy comes with the morning" (Psalm 30:5). So shed a tear with all who sorrow over the untimely deaths of their little

---

[1]For more on this subject, see my article "Where Do Babies Who Die Spend Eternity" at fbsweetwater.org/Resources/Publications.htm.

ones, but celebrate the coming of Christ and let your tears be filled with hope in the faithfulness of our Lord.

Christmas and New Year can bring a share of sorrow,
Wondering what hope can be found in tomorrow,
But where there is mourning, the Lord can turn to joy
Through the life and work of Mary's special lil' Boy.

Application Idea

What was a sad time in your life in which you have found some measure of joy? Is it the loss of a loved one who is now with the Lord? Is it a friendship or job no longer in the picture? How does sorrow-turned-to-joy give you hope for the future?

"It Came Upon the Midnight Clear"
Author: Edmund H. Sears, 1849

It came upon the midnight clear,
That glorious song of old,
From angels bending near the earth
To touch their harps of gold:
"Peace on the earth, good will to men,
From heav'n's all gracious King."
The world in solemn stillness lay
To hear the angels sing.

Still through the cloven skies they come
With peaceful wings unfurled,
And still their heavenly music floats
O'er all the weary world;
Above its sad and lowly plains,
They bend on hovering wing,
And ever over its Babel sounds
The blessed angels sing.

Yet with the woes of sin and strife
The world has suffered long,
Beneath the angel strain have rolled
Two thousand years of wrong;
And man, at war with man, hears not

The love song which they bring:
O hush the noise, ye men of strife,
And hear the angels sing!

And ye, beneath life's crushing load,
Whose forms are bending low,
Who toil along the climbing way
With painful steps and slow,
Look now! for glad and golden hours
Come swiftly on the wing:
O rest beside the weary road
And hear the angels sing!

For lo! the days are hast'ning on,
By prophet bards foretold,
When with the ever circling years
Comes round the age of gold;
When peace shall over all the earth
Its ancient splendors fling,
And the whole world give back the song
Which now the angels sing.

Prayer

Father, while I don't pretend to know all the reasons for my
sorrows in this life, I'm thankful for Your comforting grace and I'll
trust You to bring about good from the bad times in my life. I
offer this prayer in Jesus' name, Amen.

December 31   **The Child of Destiny**

My eyes have seen your salvation that you have prepared in the presence of all peoples, a light for revelation to the Gentiles, and for glory to your people Israel…. And Simeon blessed [Jesus' parents] and said to Mary his mother, "Behold, this child is appointed for the fall and rising of many in Israel, and for a sign that is opposed (and a sword will pierce through your own soul also), so that thoughts from many hearts may be revealed." (Luke 2:30-32, 34-35)

Have you ever met someone who had been destined for greatness? I've met Truett Cathy, founder of Chick-fil-A, who demonstrated a strong work ethic and sound business practices as a boy. I've read about Billy Graham and his ability to capture large audiences with his preaching. In high school I played against Scott Rolen, one of the best defensive third basemen in the history of Major League Baseball. He was gifted with extraordinary quickness and strength. Some people display certain characteristics as children, teenagers or young adults. But no one looks at a baby and sees one destined for greatness, because the child has yet to show what he/she will be like. But no child has ever been like Jesus.

Simeon, the God-fearer, saw Jesus and immediately praised God for fulfilling His promise to send the Messiah. In the Person of Jesus, God's salvation had come to the world, the light for both Gentiles and Jews. As a matter of fact, "Gentiles" comes from the Greek word *ethnos*, from which we get nations or ethnic groups. Jesus' coming wasn't merely restricted to Israel, but it also was a "light for revelation" to the nations. The nations had been in darkness, separated from God's light, until the coming of Jesus. Now God's light shines and enlightens people groups all around the world, just as God foretold through Isaiah (49:6; 55:5; 60:1-5; 61:9), picked up by Luke later through Paul's ministry (Acts 13:46-47; 26:22-23). This light not only is for revelation to the nations, but it, too, is Israel's glory, their hope as the people of God.

That news is certainly hope for the world, but Simeon wasn't finished speaking. After praising God he turned to Mary and spoke ominous words about Jesus' destiny: not everyone would welcome God's saving work in Jesus. Although God set Jesus up like a stone (cf. Isaiah 8:14-15; 28:13-16), Jews would either trip over Him and fall or build their lives on Him and rise. Jesus would divide the nation, even as a sign opposed by many. Not only would a large number of Jews reject Jesus as God's Messiah, but they would also oppose Him, contending against His very claims.

This contention over Jesus would be like a piercing sword in Mary's life, either cutting and dividing her own family (Jesus' half-siblings) or causing her deep, emotional pain. Whichever idea Luke intends, it seems clear Jesus' ministry will result in extreme sorrow for Mary. Her ultimate sorrow came in watching the Jews reject her Son and execute Him (cf. John 19:25-27).

The entire ministry of Jesus revealed where people really stood before God. Jesus' work reveals their thoughts or schemes, displaying their opposition to Jesus as opposition to God. Jesus' ministry was difficult, but it was His destiny. And believers all over the world have found their ultimate destiny in Him.

> Now here's the story you have been told to believe:
> The Son of God came as a Child to be received—
> Born in the town and line of David, mild and meek—
> He ministered to all: poor and rich, strong and weak.
> Sinless did He give His life eventually
> Only to rise from the dead victoriously.
> So turn from sin and trust in Him without delay!
> And thank God for a new year and for Christmas day!

Application Idea

What are some ways you have faced rejection for doing the right thing? How tough is it to be rejected by others for those things? How can the Lord use that in your life to make you productive for Him? What New Year's resolution might you affirm in Your stand for Jesus?

"Joy to the World! The Lord Is Come"
Author: Isaac Watts, 1719

> Joy to the world! the Lord is come;
> Let earth receive her King;
> Let every heart prepare Him room,
> And heav'n and nature sing,
> And heav'n and nature sing,
> And heav'n, and heav'n and nature sing.

Joy to the earth! the Savior reigns;
Let men their songs employ;
While fields and floods, rocks, hills, and plains
Repeat the sounding joy,
Repeat the sounding joy,
Repeat, repeat the sounding joy.

No more let sins and sorrows grow,
Nor thorns infest the ground;
He comes to make His blessings flow
Far as the curse is found,
Far as the curse is found,
Far as, far as the curse is found.

He rules the world with truth and grace
And makes the nations prove
The glories of His righteousness,
And wonders of His love,
And wonders of His love,
And wonders, wonders of His love.

Prayer

Lord, I praise You for fulfilling Your destiny by entering our world to give Your life for my sins. As You faced rejection, grant me strength in the New Year to face rejection from others as I stand with You. These things I ask in Jesus' name, Amen.

JOEL BREIDENBAUGH

ABOUT THE AUTHOR

Joel Breidenbaugh is the Senior Pastor of First Baptist Church of Sweetwater in Longwood, Florida, where he has served since 2008. He also serves as Assistant Professor of Homiletics for Liberty University School of Divinity. He has a BA in Theology from Florida Baptist Theological College, Graceville, Florida; and both the Master of Divinity and Doctor of Philosophy degrees from The Southern Baptist Theological Seminary, Louisville, Kentucky.

Joel's published writings include *Preaching for Bodybuilding: Integrating Doctrine and Expository Preaching in a Postmodern World* (2010), as well as several articles in *The Journal of Florida Baptist Heritage*, *The Popular Encyclopedia of Apologetics*, and *The Encyclopedia of Christianity in the United States* (forthcoming).

Joel's wife, Annthea, is from Bonifay, Florida. They have five children: Hannah, John Mark, Alethea, Lukas and Joanna. Joel's hobbies include reading; playing baseball and basketball; coaching his sons; watching baseball and basketball; traveling; and spending time with his family.

You may follow Joel on Twitter @DrJoelB or through his blog at www.DrJoelB.com.